Contents

Contents

Foreword

The three chapters which comprise the main text of this book (apart from three appendices), were written by me during 1983-84 for Special Numbers of *Pāñcajanya*, the Hindi weekly of the Sangh Parivar published from New Delhi. They were put together in a 40-page booklet — *Sekyularijm: Raṣṭradroha kā Dūsarā Nāma* — and published in 1985 by Bharata-Bharati, the Hindi section of Voice of India.

I retained the English term "secularism" in the Hindi title because the current Hindi terms — *dharma-nirpekṣatā, panth-nirpekṣatā, sarva-dharma-samabhāva*, etc. — did not convey the correct meaning of the English term as used in the modern West where the ideology of Secularism had taken shape during the European Enlightenment (18-19 centuries). Pandit Jawaharlal Nehru who had never used the term in his pre-independence writings or speeches, simply picked up a prestigious word from the Western political parlance and made it mean the opposite of what it meant in the West. The outcome of this perversion proved disastrous for the newly independent nation, as became more than obvious in due course. In pre-independence India, the "Muslim minority" had exercised a veto on who was to be hailed as "nationalist" and who was to be denounced as "Hindu communalist". Now the same "minority" reacquired the same veto on who was to be applauded as "secularist" and who was to be hounded out as "communalist". In short, the term "secularism" in the post-independence period has been and remains no more than a euphamism for Hindu-baiting.

But at the same time, I had made a serious mistake in using the term "secularism" as such in the title without qualifying it as "Bhārata kā" (India's). The mistake gave rise to the impression that I was opposed to Secularism in its original Western sense. I was not, as I had made quite clear in Chapter 2 of the Hindi original. The mistake has been corrected in this English translation by retitling the book as "India's Secularism". The word "India's" instead of "Indian" has been used because there is nothing Indian about Nehruvian Secularism. In fact, the term "secularism" in its original Western sense had remained unknown to Indian political parlance because Indians had never envisaged or experienced a theocratic dispensation before the advent of Islam and its state apparatus in this country. Even today, traditional Indian scholars do not understand what Theocracy means, and how Secularism in the Western sense stands opposed to it. And I did not qualify this "secularism" as Nehruvian because it is shared in common by all political parties including the Bharatiya Janata Party.

II

Some perceptive readers of the Hindi original had recognized its merit in putting the record straight, and urged upon me the need to publish an English translation without delay so that the information could reach a wider readership. But because of other and more pressing preoccupations, I could not do the translation myself. And no one else came forward to undertake the job, till I met the late Professor Suhas Majumdar for the first time during his visit to Delhi in 1992. An year or so earlier, I had been pleasantly surprised to receive a copy of *Sekyulārisjam: Raṣṭra-droher Apar Nāma*, a Bengali translation of the Hindi booklet which Shri Majumdar had published from Calcutta, all unknown to me. As we sat together for hours on end and discussed several subjects of

common interest, I discovered that Shri Majumdar was a great
scholar with as good a command over Hindi as he had over
Bengali and English. He agreed to do the English translation of
this book. But that was not to be. I gave priority to his
preparing an expanded English version of his book on *Jihād*
which had already been published in Bengali. Little did I know
that he would be struck down by cancer soon after Voice of
India published his *Jihād : The Islamic Doctrine of Permanent
War* in 1994. The world of Hindu scholarship had suffered a
great loss.

Now Shri Yashpal Sharma has done what should have been
but could not be done earlier. I have examined his translation
and found it pretty apt. What adds weight to his translation is a
compilation by him of relevant verses from the Bible and the
Quran as well as precedent from the Sunnah of the Prophet of
Islam, which sanction the behaviour pattern of the followers of
Christianity and Islam towards those they denounce as
"infidels". This behaviour pattern has been detailed in the
main text of this book, and Shri Sharma thought it fit to show
that the behaviour pattern is neither an accident of history nor
the outcome of normal human nature, but follows logically
and inevitably from doctrines laid down in the sacred
scriptures of these creeds.

Herculean efforts have been made and are being made by
the apologists of Christianity and Islam in modern times, to
salvage the central figures and fundamental doctrines of these
creeds from the blood-soaked histories they have enacted for
many years in many parts of the world. The apologists have
been trying to prove that the inhuman atrocities with which
these histories are brimful, have nothing to do with their sacred
scriptures and can be explained "more satisfactorily" in terms
of the human infirmities of persons or peoples who committed
the atrocites. In post-independence India, this Christian and
Islamic Apologetics has achieved remarkable success, so
much so that while these creeds pass as advocates of human
brotherhood, social justice, human rights, freedom, equality,

peace, and progress, their doctrines and doings have been projected on to Hinduism and Hindu history by a motley crowd of "secularists" spawned by Socialism, Communism, Gandhism, Nehruism, Ambedkarism, etc. Shri Sharma has nailed the lies by quoting chapter and verse from the sacred scriptures of Christianity and Islam. His compilation can be read in Appendix 3 of this book.

The book carries two more appendices. Appendix 1 is the text of a speech — The Emerging National Vision — which I had delivered on 4 December 1983 under the auspices of Yogakshema, Calcutta. The speech was published as a booklet at the end of December 1983, and reprinted in December 1984 and December 1986. The booklet has been out of print for quite some time. Appendix 2 is the text of a letter which Shri Baljit Rai, erudite scholar of Chandigarh, had addressed on 5 December 1998 to the University Grants Commission as well as the Vice-Chancellors of all mainstream universities in India, pleading that study of Islamic Polity be introduced in departments of Political Science so that our younger generations may know how Islam has treated non-Muslims throughout its history and what its theology continues to prescribe even today.

Political developments in India in recent years indicate that a National Vision *is* emerging in the Hindu intelligentsia at large. The pace of this emergence is slow because old slogans continue to dominate the media and the academia. It will take some time for these slogans to get exhausted. The world at large is realizing the danger which Islamic terrorism poses to peace and progress, and we too will have to face the truth.

We have been fighting Islamic terrorism in its latest manifestation over the last more than two decades. But the ideology which inspires that terrorism, namely, Islam, has been ignored by our mainstream universities. Islamic Studies have remained a close preserve of a few mainstream universities like the Aligarh Muslim University and the Jamia Millia Islamia at New Delhi. Meanwhile, fundamentalist

Islamic seminaries like the Dar-ul-Uloom at Deoband (U.P.), have multiplied. Neither these Muslim universities nor these Islamic seminaries can be expected to present Islam from a secular-humanist point of view.

This book is going to the printing press simultaneously with the Third Revised and Enlarged Edition of *The Calcutta Quran Petition*. The two books are companion volumes.

New Delhi
31.7.1999

Sita Ram Goel

Chapter – 1

What is Dharma?

When the European scholars in 18-19th centuries (CE) began to translate the literature of India in their own languages, they felt a special difficulty with regard to one word. That word was 'dharma'. In European languages, there was no one word which could completely express the essential nature of dharma. So the European scholars had to make use of different words relative to the context in which the word had been used in Indian literature. In the English language, dharma was translated as religion, righteousness, law, tradition, moral code, etc., according to the context. Thus European scholars confirmed that great saying of Bhishma Pitamaha in the Mahabharata: "धर्मस्य गहना गति:" (the dynamics of dharma is deep).

But the modern scholars in India did not have to experience any such difficulty in the context of translation. They heard the word 'religion' of the English language and decided instantly and unanimously that this word should be translated as 'dharma' in all Indian languages.

The performance was very economical, so that all the sects of Sanatana Dharma — Smarta, Jaina, Bauddha, Shaiva, Vaishnava, Shakta, Saurya, Ganapatya, Siddha and Santa — on the one side, and Islam and Christianity on the other, were brought within the circumference of one common denomination — dharma.

Among the schools of Sanatana Dharma, the tradition of mutual tolerance and equal regard was as old as the schools themselves. This tradition was now extended to Islam and Christianity without any doubt or hesitation. This extension (of equal regard) was quite correct from the Sanatana Dharma point of view, if Islam and Christianity were dharmas similar to the dharmas of the schools of the Sanatana Dharma.

But Christian theologians and missionaries and the ulema and mullahs of Islam could not wholly agree to this reciprocal exchange of equal regard. They liked it very much that the schools of Sanatana Dharma cultivate respect towards their religions, but they could not agree to the proposition that their own religions should manifest reciprocal regard for Sanatana Dharma or for any of its schools.

Christian theologians and missionaries said that all schools of Sanatana Dharma carry the message of Satan, and that they did not conform to the divine message given by Jesus Christ. Muslim ulema and mullahs gave fatwas that all schools of Sanatana Dharma were *kufr* and had nothing in common with the unique revelation from Allah, conveyed through Prophet Muhammad.

The demand of discrimination was to find out a solution to this dilemma. An attempt should have been made to know why Islam and Christianity had nothing in common with Sanatana Dharma. But Indian scholars paid no heed to the statements from the spokesmen for Christianity and Islam. These scholars contented themselves with this much only that the scriptures of Islam and Christianity contained some sentences which sounded consistent with Sanatana Dharma. And by publishing collections of such stray sentences with their own comments, these scholars proclaimed that they were experts on Islam and Christianity as well.

It is needless to say that this was a presumptuous attempt the evil consequences of which the Hindu society has had to suffer. The more strongly the Hindu society pronounces its goodwill towards Islam and Christianity, the more sharply increases Islam's persistence to convert India into *dār al-Islām* (the land of Islam), and Christianity's harangue that until India becomes the land of Jesus, India's salvation is impossible.

In this situation, the right course is that expositions of Islam and Christianity be heard from the mouths of their own spokesmen, and then alone a decision be taken whether, in the context of their religions, the notion of equal regard towards them is justified or not. The Hindu society should shed the illusion that it alone is competent to speak on behalf of all other societies.

The Two Traditions of Worship

History stands witness that both Islam and Christianity have been in conflict not only with Sanatana Dharma but also with many other ways of worship which have flourished outside India. In fact, conflict with regard to mode of worship commenced with the emergence of that psyche which Christianity and Islam carry within them. Before the rise of Christianity, no trace of any bloodshed regarding mode of worship can be found in the history of the world. With the advent of Islam, even those areas of the world were also drenched in blood where the sword of Christianity had not reached. Therefore, first of all we should get acquainted with the psyche of Christianity and Islam, and then compare that psyche with the other psyche which has been nourished in those traditions of worship which have been destroyed by Christianity and Islam or which they want to destroy.

A bird's-eye view of the history of the world tells us that there have been two traditions of worship. We will call one the tradition of Advaita, and the other that of Monotheism.

The tradition of Advaita is found prevalent particularly in the ancient cultures of India, Iran, Egypt, Greece, Rome, China and Japan. Before the spread of Christianity, the Celt, German, Frank, Slav and Scandinavian peoples of Europe were also followers of Advaita. In the cultures of the original inhabitants of South and North America, the stamp of Advaita is clearly visible. In those communities of Africa also which have not yet been converted to Christianity or Islam, consciousness of Advaita exists. In ancient Ethiopia, the shape of Advaita was sufficiently refined.

On the other hand, Monotheism rose first of all among the Jews who, after a long spell of nomadic life, had settled down in Palestine. A detailed exposition as well as the history of their Monotheism is available in the Old Testament of the Bible. Among them was born Jesus whom some of his disciples proclaimed as the 'Christ' after his death. Christianity's exposition is available in the New Testament of the Bible. After organising a powerful Church, Christianity seized the Roman Empire in the fourth century (CE). That empire had expanded far and wide in Europe, West Asia and North Africa. Thereafter, Christianity spread in other parts of Europe from the fifth to the fifteenth century and, by the beginning of the sixteenth century, Christianity along with European imperialism reached the countries of America, Africa and Asia. Many countries among them became completely christianized. Now this faith is steadily spreading in the other countries.

The rise of Islam occurred in the first half of the seventh century (CE). This faith had spread in its birthplace, Arabia, in the life-time of its founder, Muhammad. Thereafter, Arab armies carried Islam upto Spain through North Africa on the one side, and to Syria, Palestine, Iraq, Iran, Khurasan, Central Asia and Sindh on the other. The armies of Turkish imperialism strived for several hundred years to spread Islam in Europe on the one hand and in India on the other. In Europe, this effort (to spread Islam) remained wholly unsuccessful except in some regions, so much so that the well-established rule of Islam in Spain was also uprooted. But in India, Islam gained significant success. The present-day Afghanistan, Pakistan and Bangladesh, once parts of India, are the living examples of that success. In addition to this, in Indonesia, Malaysia and several countries of Africa, Islam has spread its tentacles far and wide.

Spread of Faith and Use of Force

In the tradition of Advaita, one characteristic is particularly noteworthy. In the long history of this tradition, not a single instance of spread of faith by use of force is available. Among the countries and communities following the tradition of Advaita, many wars have been fought due to many kinds of differences and hostilities. But never has any war been fought for the spread of faith. In this context, the spread of Buddhism is particularly notable. In the spread of this dharma, not a single soldier ever played any role. The monks of the Dharma Sangha alone carried this faith far and wide. And in the countries where Buddhism spread, it never came into conflict with the ancient modes of worship prevalent in those countries.

On the other hand, the whole history of the spread of Monotheism is the history of use of force in various ways. The expansion of Christianity and Islam took place only through the use of armed force or economic power or a combination both, by some imperialism or the other. In the process of this expansion, three facts stare us in the face:

Firstly, the followers of Monotheism destroyed the religious places of other faiths, broke or defiled the sacred images of their gods, burnt their sacred scriptures, killed their priests and saints or dishonoured them, and made untiring efforts to destroy their cultures, root and branch.

Secondly, the Monotheists converted the followers of other faiths at the point of the sword or by tempting them with money or privilege or by humiliating them in other ways.

Thirdly, the Monotheists slaughtered in cold blood the defeated warriors of other faiths, enslaved and sold their innocent families in far-off lands, and plundered all their movable, immovable and other properties. Those followers of the other faiths who still survived after all this mayhem, were made second class citizens, burdened with many disabilities and trodden under foot in various ways by the Monotheists in power.

The apologists of Christianity and Islam attribute the blame for these horrors of history to the innate barbarism of this or that conqueror tribe, and pronounce that in principle there is no place for use of force in Monotheistic faiths. And in support of this contention, these scholars quote a few lines from the Bible or the Quran. Hindu exponents of *sarva-dharma-samabhāva* never tire of supporting this apologetics. Therefore, it is a subject for enquiry as to how much substance there is in this apologetics. History stands witness that whenever and wherever the followers of Monotheism have used force, its use has been openly praised by their clerics and historians. They state quite clearly that the use of force is sanctioned by their religion, and quote the relevant command-ments from their scriptures.

At the same time, we have to see as to why, in the traditions of Advaita, there is no provision for use of force for spreading faith.

Examination of Advaita Spirituality

In many countries of the world, the traditions of Advaita have been completely destroyed by Christianity and Islam. Only some surviving literature of ancient Iran, Egypt, Greece and Rome contains exposition of Advaita, clear or confused. It is only in India, Sri Lanka, Burma, Thailand, South Korea and Japan that the tradition has survived intact to a large extent. A substantial exposition of the material that can be collected from all these sources, is now available only in India. Therefore, it is with the help of that exposition that we will make a presentation of Advaita.

The very first proposition that is immediately visible in all schools of Advaita, is polytheism. In no school of Advaita is seen any special emphasis on some God as the creator or controller of the Cosmos. Contrary to this, many mythologies have grown around numerous gods and goddesses. In some mythology one particular god or goddess is installed as the supreme object of worship, and in another some other god or goddess. And whatever god is installed at any time as the supreme object of worship, all other gods and goddesses get merged in him or her. One might say that each god or goddess is an image of all the other gods and goddesses. In the schools of Sanatana Dharma, several gods and goddesses are known by a thousand names. This also is a clear indication that all gods and goddesses are symbols of one infinite, ineffable and indescribable supreme power. In the words of Tulsidas, हरि अनन्त हरिकथा अनन्ता (God is infinite, so also the narratives in his praise).

The second proposition that is there in all schools of Advaita, is that gods and goddesses may assume any animate or inanimate form. Several gods and goddesses are found in the form of a human-male or a human-female or in their pair. Many gods and goddesses are worshipped in the form of animals, birds, aquatic creatures, rivers, mountains, plants, trees, etc. All these gods and goddesses are worshipped as carved images. Many a time, uncarved stones also become objects worship. This is a clear indication of the truth that the entire animate and inanimate creation is pervaded by one Being, and a devotee can worship that Being in any form. And there is also found in the tradition of Advaita, a provision for worship of the Formless which is beyond all forms.

The third proposition that is found in all schools of Advaita, is that there are many ways of worship. The same god can be worshipped in various ways. Consequently, there is an abundance of schools in this tradition. Every now and then, new schools arise, develop, merge with some pre-existing school, and also vanish. In this tradition, what holds primacy is not the object of worship or the mode of worship, but the devotion in the act of worship. The object of worship or mode of worship can never be at fault. The fault can lie only in the quality of devotion. In the words of Tulsidas, जाकी रही भावना जैसी, प्रभु मूरत देखी तिन तैसी (the level of one's devotion determines the form in which one sees God). Therefore, the worshipper bears only the responsibility for his own conduct and thought; to watch the conduct and thought of others or to preach uninvited to others, is not countenanced in this tradition. In the words of Kabirdas, बुरा जो देखन मैं चला बुरा न दीखा कोय, जो दिल खोजा आपना मुझसा बुरा न कोय (as I went out in search the bad one, I found none; but when I examined my own self, I found that no one was worse than myself). Far from using force for the spread of faith, even to be concerned with the conduct and thought of others, indicates a fall from faith.

The fourth proposition that is found in the tradition of Advaita, is that truth is eternal and impersonal. Realization of truth is not the monopoly any particular person, nor can it be borrowed from any other person. Any seeker who searches for truth in any place or at any time, finds it in full. Truth is not the fragmented pieces revealed progressively in chronological time; nor does truth ever become brand new. The language or style of expressing that truth may be novel. But if any person claims that he has searched for or found or seen or heard a truth the like of which no other person has ever known before, then in the tradition of Advaita he is considered a liar and a victim of delusion. Buddha had said, "I have become the Enlightened one by walking on the same path on which the Enlightened Ones preceding me had walked, and the succeeding Enlightened Ones will walk."

The fifth proposition that is found in the tradition of Advaita, is that man should not hold any belief which is not consistent with reason from the very beginning and which is not verifiable ultimately at some level of human consciousness. An inference which fails the test of direct perception ultimately, has very little value. The word 'śabda-pramāṇa' which is found in the Shastras of Advaita tradition, is a synonym for direct perception: śabda-pramāṇa, that is, the proof which the accomplished persons have themselves found thorough spiritual seeking and, thereafter, placed before others. If we cannot test directly the teachings of Sri Krishna or Buddha or some other avatar or spiritually perfect person, by ascending into the highest consciousness of those great ones, then those teachings are meaningless for us — ऋषयः मन्त्रदृष्टारः (the Rishis are seers of what the mantras symbolize).

The sixth proposition that is found in the tradition of Advaita, is that of *vasudhaiva kutumbakam,* that is, the whole of humanity is a single family, and everyone of its members deserves and should manifest the same considerate conduct from and towards all others. The scope of considerate conduct is not confined to any one particular sect or community. So no person or sect or community should do unto others what he or she or it does not like to be done unto him or her or it — श्लोकार्धेन प्रवक्ष्यामि यदुक्तं ग्रंथकोटिभिः, आत्मनः प्रतिकूलानि परेषां न समाचरेत (I state in half a couplet what has been said in a million treatises: Do not do unto others what you find unpalatable for yourself).

The seventh proposition that is found in the tradition of Advaita, is that while it concedes the superiority of humans it does not consider other parts of creation as objects of human consumption. The view that is fostered in a devotee of Advaita, is that all that is there in the universe, animate or inanimate, manifests different limbs of the One Vast Being and, while using those limbs for sustenance and right livelihood, a feeling of friendship should be cultivated towards all of them. Human superiority lies only in this much that birth as a human being facilitates the attainment of supreme truth. In the words of Tulsidas, human birth is साधन धाम मोक्षकर द्वारा (field for spiritual seeking and gateway to final emancipation). Man in his ordinary state is not the master of the universe. Man should consider himself indebted for all the help and cooperation he gets from various components of the universe for his subsistence and his physical, intellectual and spiritual development. And man should repay these debts according to his opportunity and capacity. The Hindu doctrine of repaying the five debts — to rishis, ancestors, gods, humans, all other animate and inanimate creatures — is expressive of the same principle.

In brief, the tradition of Advaita is empirical, rational, and spiritual. The first aphorism of the esoteric presentation of that tradition is यथा पिण्डे तथा ब्रह्माण्डे (as in the microcosm, so in the macrocosm), that is, by exploring the individual self, the secret of the universe can be discovered. Or in other words, सर्व निवासी सदा अलेपा, तोहे संग समाई (the eternally transcendent which is immanent in all, dwells within you). Greek thinkers say that "man is the measure of all things", that is, man is the key for understanding everything else. It is only by grasping this truth that the author of the Mahabharata says — गुह्यं ब्रह्म तदिदं वो ब्रवीमि, न हि मानुषात् श्रेष्ठतरं हि किंचित् (I tell you the great secret: There is nothing superior to man). In the words of Chandidas, सबार ऊपर मानुष सत्य (man is the truth above all other truths).

It is because of an appropriate knowledge of this secret, that the tradition of Advaita does not keep repeating ad nauseam the name of any One God who is extra-cosmic and who is not directly accessible to by all human beings. The human soul in its secret depths is the Supreme Soul. The human person, when purified, becomes the Perfect Person. A seeker of Advaita, after becoming spiritually perfect, says — सर्व खल्विदं ब्रह्म (all this in the Vast), तत्त्वमसि (thou art That), अहं ब्रह्मास्मि (I am the Vast). Buddha had even abandoned the philosophy centered round Soul and God or Being and Becoming. This philosophy is likely to end in casuistry.

Hence, the tradition of Advaita is fully humanistic. The supreme truth is surely eternal and impersonal, but it is attainable by every person. Each person is a field for spiritual seeking, is a *bodhisattva*. A person, after becoming perfect through spiritual seeking, ascends into the same supreme consciousness, on being established in which, Sri Krishna came to be known as Purushottama (the Perfect Person), and Sakyamuni as Samyak Sambuddha (the Perfectly Enlightened). But each person has to seek for himself. Spiritual attainment cannot be borrowed from any messiah or prophet. No prophet can, by recommending a person, send him to heaven, nor can that prophet, on being angry with any person, push him into hell. In fact, the whole story of heaven and hell is meant to deceive children. For each person, the inevitable destiny is Nirvana, Moksha, the attainment of Paramapada (the highest station), and enjoyment of bliss in all its infinities. And for advancing towards that destiny, a person need not become impatient. According to his own aptitude and in keeping with his spiritual development, whatever spiritual merit a person earns in one birth, that becomes his capital for further progress in the next birth. And this spiritual striving, practised through many births, continues till a person attains the perfect truth and himself becomes that truth.

Fundamentals of Monotheism

Monotheism has three sects — Judaism, Christianity and Islam. These three sects are scions of the same mother. They are born out of same psyche, and the main mythical and doctrinal propositions of all the three are similar. Therefore, first of all, we will describe the propositions shared in common by these three faiths.

The first proposition of Monotheism is that the creator and controller of the Cosmos is the One God who is unique, who does not manifest himself in different forms, and who does not permit the worship of any god or goddess other than himself. There is no element outside or inside the Cosmos which is of the same substance as the One God, or is his part, or is pervaded by him. Therefore, to worship any other gods or goddesses or to regard any part of the Cosmos as divine, is a serious crime against the One God.

The second proposition of Monotheism is that the One God has created the Cosmos without the aid of any substance, that is, out of sheer Void or Nothing. This miracle is indicative of the omnipotence of the One God. If the One God had taken the least aid from any substance, his omnipotence would have suffered disparagement. For this very reason, he himself also remained outside of his own creation.

The third proposition of Monotheism is that the human male

is the highest creation of the One God. At the time of creating the human male, the One God made a clay figure of the human form and blew his own breath into it. This breath became the soul of the human male. Monotheism is not quite sure whether the human female has a soul or not. The One God had taken one rib out of the human male and carved it into a figure of the human female without blowing his breath into that figure. Nor can human soul be regarded as a divine entity. After acquiring the soul, the human being became conscious and capable of thinking and also attained the capacity to distinguish between vice and virtue. But this soul cannot be considered a part of the One God. Monotheism is also quite clear that all other animate and inanimate parts of creation have been created merely for enjoyment by humans, and humans should not harbour any other feeling towards them.

According to the fourth proposition of Monotheism, man has only one life and the supreme elevation of that life is an exclusive worship of the One God. An indispensable part of that worship is that man regulates all his conduct and thought in accordance with the commandments of the One God. But man cannot acquaint himself with those commandments by establishing direct contact with the One God. The One God remains outside the Cosmos while man remains inside it. Therefore, direct contact between the two is inconceivable. Thus finding man groping in the dark, the One God takes pity on him and, in order to convey his commandments to man, he sends his prophets from time to time. Every commandment of the One God revealed by each prophet is unprecedented; it had never been heard before. In this process of history, the One God at last sends his perfect prophet through whose mouth a comprehensive and complete code of commandments of the One God is received by man. This prophet is called the Last Prophet who pronounces the final commandments of the One God, to which nothing can be added and from which nothing can be subtracted. In the revelations by the Last Prophet, the whole truth is incorporated.

According to the fifth proposition of Monotheism, two events take place after the advent of the Last Prophet. Firstly, the history of mankind gets divided into two periods. The period before the coming of the Last Prophet, becomes the period of darkness or ignorance, and the period thereafter the period of light or knowledge. No mode of worship or cultural heritage or social custom of the earlier period, remains valid and a complete destruction of whatever prevailed earlier, is considered conducive to salvation of mankind. Secondly, after the coming of the Last Prophet, mankind is divided into two groups. One group is that which professes complete faith in the Last Prophet and begins to follow the path shown by him. The other group is that which professes doubts regarding the Last Prophet or repudiates him. The first group becomes dear to the One God, and the second invites his wrath. The One God commands the first group to wage ceaseless jihad against the second group, and either make that group submit to the Last Prophet or annihilate it altogether.

The sixth proposition of Monotheism is that the One God has bestowed sovereignty of the whole world on his Last Prophet, and the Last Prophet on the group professing complete faith in him. At the same time, the One God has confiscated the lives and properties of the group which rebels against his Last Prophet. Therefore, the believing group has the sacred duty to obey his commandments and seize the lives and properties of the rebel group. Those of the rebel group who take to arms in their defence, should be massacred. Their families should be captured and sold into slavery. Their movable and immovable properties should be plundered. Their religious places should be destroyed. Their religious books should be burnt. Their saints and sages and priests should be dishonoured if not killed outright. And their whole cultural wealth should be obliterated. Those of the rebel group who accept defeat, should be converted to the faith of the conqueror. If for any reason their conversion is not possible, they should be made second class citizens and oppressed till they seek refuge in the Last Prophet. In order to carry out the commandments of the One God in the context of the rebel group, it is not required that the moral character of the believing group be higher or their consciousness purer. Professing exclusive faith in the Last Prophet is enough for them. (See Appendix 3 for the scriptural sanctions which Monotheism provides for this behaviour pattern).

According to the seventh proposition of Monotheism, on the Last Day, all those born and dead from the beginning to end of creation, will rise from their graves and present themselves before the One God for his Last Judgement. On that day, the Last Prophet will reappear, sit on the right side of the One God, and give account of the good and bad deeds of each human being. Those who had professed faith in the Last Prophet will be sent to an everlasting heaven where all the objects of enjoyment of the terrestrial world will continue to be available for ever in their highest quality and limitless quantity. On the other hand, those who had rebelled against the Last Prophet will be thrown into an everlasting hell with full arrangements for subjecting them to indescribable torments. In the context of heaven and hell, it is to be noted that at the time of delivering his judgement, the One God will pay attention not to the conduct of the applicants but to their faith. Intense faith in the Last Prophet, will enable the One God to forgive many faults of conduct. The Last Prophet will also not falter in recommending favours for those devoted to him exclusively.

All these seven proposition are shared in common by Judaism, Christianity and Islam. The conflict among these three creeds is regarding the Last Prophet, leaving aside a few other secondary matters. The Jews believe in Moses as their Last Prophet, the Christians in Jesus Christ, and Muslims in Muhammad. Much maligning and also killing has taken place among these three creeds due to this conflict. The greatest sufferers have been the Jews whom Christians and Muslims call killers of prophets and corrupters of scriptures. Many holy wars have also been fought between Christianity and Islam. But in spite of these mutual differences, the followers of all these three faiths have displayed the same hostility against the followers of Advaita. Slaughters made by the Jews could not spread outside Palestine for various reasons. But the Christians and the Muslims have painted many countries with extensive bloodshed and destroyed the spiritual and cultural wealth of those countries as far as they could.

Examination of Monotheism

Firstly, Monotheism presents no proof in support of any of its propositions. All its arguments are specimens of round about logic. Existence of the One God is accepted because the prophet testifies to that existence. But the status of the prophet is hailed because he claims that the One God speaks through him. If the exponents of Monotheism are asked whether any other person can, by spiritual seeking, attain that state of consciousness by attaining which the prophet had heard the commandments of the One God, they unanimously denounce it as inconceivable. Nor do they concede to any other person the capacity to see the One God directly by any method of spiritual seeking. To meet the One God directly is not possible for any other person before the Day of Judgement. Again, it all depends upon the sweet will of the One God as to when and whom he may send as his prophet. In the history of Monotheism, it has happened many a time that persons more than one proclaimed themselves as prophets. Their dispute could be settled only when one of them killed the others or got himself killed. In this situation, it cannot be decided whether the One God that the prophet has been raving about, has any real existence or not. Nor can it be said that the command-ments which the prophet has issued in the name of the One God are not the ravings of his own mind. In this context, the tradition of Monotheism is wholly contrary to the tradition of

Advaita, which regards direct perception as the only proof, and which gives equal right to all humans to realize the supreme truth directly.

Secondly, Monotheism recognizes truth not as eternal but as the latest. The truth that the prophet reveals thorough his sayings and, doings was not known to anyone before his advent. This definition of truth can only be termed as downright ridiculous. And when it is said that truth has become complete after the advent of the Last Prophet and that nothing can be added to or subtracted from it, then this definition contradicts itself. Truth, if it is the latest, cannot be complete till the end of time. And when countless persons born before the Last Prophet or in his time or after him, are pushed into hell simply because they have failed to profess faith in the Last Prophet, then Monotheism has to be termed as vile. All these persons could not hear the message of the Last Prophet because either they were born before him or because no mullah or missionary could reach them. How can these persons be blamed for the offence of disregarding the Last Prophet? In this context, the tradition of Monotheism is wholly contrary to the tradition of Advaita, which regards truth as eternal and equally accessible to all persons at all times and at all places.

Thirdly, Monotheism regards truth not as impersonal but as personal. The prophet alone is the person who can know or hear the truth. All other persons have to borrow that truth from the prophet and practise it as such. Consequently, the prophet very soon usurps the place of the One God. Without submission to the prophet, worship of the One God is not possible. Nor can the gates of heaven open without recommendation from the prophet. In this situation, it should not be a matter of surprise if the One God takes leave or is left out. This is the inevitable transformation of Monotheism. In this context, the tradition of Monotheism is wholly contrary to the tradition of Advaita, which regards truth as impersonal and admits that जिन खोजा तिन पाइयां (whoever seeks, he finds).

Fourthly, Monotheism renders the supreme power impotent and the entire Cosmos an extension of matter. The One God, intoxicated as he was with his omnipotence, did create the universe out of Nothing or the Void, but, for the same reason, he himself remained outside his own creation. He became incapable of establishing contact with his own creatures and, in order to convey his message to human beings created by himself, he had to seek the help of a prophet. To describe such a helpless One God as almighty, is ridiculous. This debasement of the One God is surpassed by the debasement of his creation. As a consequence of the One God remaining outside, whatever there is in the Cosmos is material and man has unhindered right to use it all. Therefore, with the decline of Christianity in the Western countries, there erupted a volcano of materialism and consumerism. The natural resources began to be ruthlessly exploited. The incurable epidemic of consumerism which is pushing the word towards destruction today, had its seed in the Monotheism of Christianity. Islam followed the same path. In this context, the tradition of Monotheism is wholly contrary to the tradition of Advaita, which sees extension of the same divinity in all animate and inanimate beings and imposes limits on consumption.

Fifthly, the Supreme Being of Monotheism (whether Jehova or Allah) comes out as a despot who is also an arbitrary, partisan, and jealous gangster. If the sayings and doings which have been sanctioned in the various scriptures of Monotheism as commandments of the One God, really emanate from that One God, then there remains no scope for doubt that the One God is simply another name for Satan described in those very scriptures. That is why the devotees of the One God invoke him while committing all those atrocities which are described in detail in the history of creeds professing Monotheism. In this context, the tradition of Monotheism is wholly contrary to the tradition of Advaita, which regards the Supreme Being as Sacchidananda — Truth, Consciousness and Bliss —, the saviour of the virtuous and the purifier of the sinful.

Sixthly, by dividing human history into two periods and the human race into two mutually hostile groups, Monotheism gives to one group the right to destroy, without any compunction, the cultural wealth of the other group, slaughter that group mercilessly, grab its properties, and bind it into bonds of slavery. In fact, the ideology of Monotheism is replete with an unquenchable barbarism the explosion of which has been witnessed time and again, and in consequence of which the progress of human civilization and culture has been greatly impeded. Monotheism rationalizes the animal drives present in human nature. It is not an accident that whenever and wherever Monotheism has held sway, then and there an unbridled devil dance of evil has been enacted. The story of crimes committed under the auspices of Monotheism is exceedingly long. In this context, the tradition of Monotheism is wholly contrary to the tradition of Advaita, which protects the precious cultural wealth accumulated in the course of time, and promotes the attitude of *vasudhaiva kuṭumbakam* (the whole world is one fraternity).

Lastly, it has to be said that Monotheism, by smothering diversity in belief and behaviour of people, fosters uniformity. To describe this uniformity as universality, is the dreadful mistake that every kind of Monotheism has committed. Monotheism fails to understand that there are many regions, many countries, many races, and countless human beings with different natures and temperaments. It prescribes a uniform pattern of belief and behaviour for all countries, for all times, for all races, and for all persons. Monotheism fails to see whether all men are capable of living up to that pattern of belief and behaviour, or not. Moreover, for practising that uniform pattern, man has got only one life. If in that one life a man fails to live up to that pattern, then he is consigned to an everlasting hell. Monotheism has not given any opportunity to any one to rectify one's mistake. In this context, the tradition of Monotheism is wholly contrary to the tradition of Advaita, which provides for diversity of belief and behaviour in accordance with the stage of a man's spiritual development and aptitude and which, affirming that each man is a *bodhisattva*, gives an opportunity to him for spiritual seeking through a cycle of rebirths.

In brief, the tradition of Advaita regards direct perception as the only proof of its propositions, whether that direct perception be through the senses or extra-sensory. The tradition of Advaita regards truth as eternal and impersonal, and grants to everyone the right to approach truth direct. This tradition sees the Supreme Truth manifest in many forms outside as well as inside the Cosmos, provides for different ways of worship, holds behaviour superior to belief, denounces use of force for spreading of faith, does not rationalize any animal drive present in human nature, promotes many cultures in accordance with time and place, and repudiates all kinds of imperialism.

On the other hand, the tradition of the Monotheism is not based on any kind of positive proof, regards truth as new and personal, describes its One God as unique and outside the Cosmos, provides for only one pattern of belief and behaviour by presenting the Last Prophet as the ideal person, holds belief superior to behaviour, gives validity to use of force for spreading the faith, rationalizes all kinds of animal drives present in human nature, and encourages imperialistic ambitions.

In the end, one clarification is desirable. The above analysis of Advaita and Monotheism is wholly right at the level of ideas. But this analysis cannot be applied mechanically to all persons born and brought up in these opposite traditions. The head and heart of a person can be larger or smaller than any thought pattern. Unless a person brought up and bred in any tradition accepts that tradition consciously and begins to imbibe and promote it, the tradition does not become manifest in his life. It is not enough to merely mouth support for any pattern of belief and behaviour. Therefore, ordinary men born and brought up in both the traditions are found to be of good as well as bad behaviour. Differences arise when different individuals espouse the opposite traditions of Advaita and

Monotheism intellectually and cherish them consciously. Then the tradition of Monotheism gives birth to Aurangzeb, and the tradition of Advaita to Shivaji.

Chapter – 2

Secularism: Perversion of Meaning

There is a famous adage — कौवा चला हंस की चाल, अपनी भी भूल गया (the crow tried to walk like the swan, but ended by forgetting its own way of walking). Such a transformation is considered crazy, but not calamitous. But when a swan forgets its own identity and begins to ape a crow, then a terrible tragedy takes place. In this hallowed land of Sanatana Dharma where, before the advent of Islam, there had never been any bloodshed in the name of dharma, we have only invited great trouble for ourselves by importing the alien concept of Secularism from Europe.

Perversion of Meaning in Translation

In the ethos and history of Europe, many concepts have originated and developed which we cannot understand without a proper study of that ethos and history. When we adopt those concepts by translating them literally or even substantially in our own language and make them current in our country which has had a different ethos and history, then we not only render those concepts invalid but also corrupt and obscure the heritage of our culture. The concept of Secularism which we have made current in our politics by calling it *dharmanirpekṣhtā or sarva-dharma-samabhāva*, is one such concept.

The ideology which was propagated and spread and made known as religion in the history of Europe after the rise of

Christianity, is not traceable in the history of India before the advent of Islam and Christianity in this country. And the dharmic ethos which had prevailed in this country for ages past during the pre-Islamic period, is not found in the history of Europe after the rise of Christianity. Therefore, in order to avoid the perversion of meaning arising from translation, we are using the word 'secularism' itself in this book. We cannot find any word in Indian languages which can convey the correct meaning of this alien concept.

Secularism: Rise and Development

In the countries of Europe, after the fourth and before the eighteenth century (CE), there was a strong bond between the Christian Church and the State. The function of the State was not only to supervise and control the worldly (secular) life of its subjects, but also to secure their salvation in the next world. The key to salvation in the next world was in possession of the Church. But if any citizen disregarded or violated the rules of conduct proclaimed by the Church from time to time, the Church pleaded that it was incapable of inflicting physical punishment on him. The Church used to excommunicate him and thus close the gate of heaven for him. Thereafter, it was the duty of the State to burn that man alive or kill him by means of other tortures or throw him into prison. Besides this, in most countries of Europe, there were Jews whom the Church had stigmatized as the "killers of Christ". The Jews had been deprived of all citizenship rights. Even so, from time to time, the State inflicted many atrocities on them on orders from the Church, or fanatic Christian mobs subjected the Jewish settlements to repeated rounds of terror and gangster-ism without any fear of the State. Hence, in the language of the Church, the State was termed the "secular arm" of the Church, and the State also admitted publicly that its main function was to serve the Church.

So long as the continent of Europe retained communities which were yet to be converted to Christianity, cooperation between the Church and the State continued smoothly. The Church had given absolute liberty to the kings to expand their domains in the name of spreading Christianity. The kings also used the sword, as far as practicable, for converting the non-Christians to Christianity or for slaughtering them or for trampling them under foot in other ways. The Church applauded the kings wholeheartedly for their services. In turn, the kings also claimed that they were striving heart and soul in order to save the pagans from hell-fire. In this sinister alliance, both the kings and the Church extended their dominions and domination. Dissensions also cropped up between the two from time to time, but cooperation was so beneficial that conflicts continued to be resolved.

Thereafter, a time came at the end of the fifteenth century when the whole of Europe became Christianized. The kings were no more in need of blessings from the Church in order to augment their power. The State began to feel restless against the stranglehold which the Church had imposed on it. In the sixteenth century, widespread revolts broke out against the Church and Christianity got splintered into several sects. But the reformist sects of Christianity proved to be far more intolerant, and a terrible carnage took place all over Europe in the name of religion. The State in one country, by aligning with one sect, began to suppress the other sects, while the State in another country, by aligning with another sect, began to suppress all others. And wars began to be fought among different countries in the name of religion.

Fortunately for Europe, during that very period, the leading thinkers of Europe had come in contact with some ancient cultures. Among these cultures, the culture of ancient Greece was the foremost. These thinkers also learnt much from the ancient cultures of India and China. And influenced by the humanism, rationalism and universalism inherent in these cultures, they revolted against Christianity. Christianity did not have the capacity to pass the test posed by reason, and before long the whole mumbo-jumbo of Christianity crumbled. At the end of the eighteenth century, along with the French Revolution, this process got accelerated.

This was the background in which Secularism arose in Europe. In the nineteenth century, the State was liberated from the stranglehold of the Church in every country in Europe. It was no longer the function of the State to secure salvation for its citizens. To seek and strive for salvation in the next world or not, became now the personal concern of each citizen. The State had now no concern with the personal belief or unbelief of a citizen. To supervise and regulate the conduct of a citizen in this world alone, remained the function of the State. The State, thus freed from the stranglehold of the Church, became known as the Secular State, and gradually Europe evolved a culture which repudiated all sorts of religious fanaticism.

Relevance of Secularism in India

At the time of independence, there existed in India also two forms of that ideology tormented by which Europe had adopted the concept of Secularism. One form of that ideology was Islam and the other Christianity. Islam which came into this country with alien imperialism, had made unbridled use of state power for several hundred years (like Christianity in Europe) in order to sustain its gangsterism, and divided the country eventually. Likewise, Christianity also used state power in order to commit all sorts of atrocities for its propagation and expansion in the region of Goa and elsewhere in the sixteenth century. The British rule also would have carried out similar sinister schemes, had it not freed itself from the stranglehold of Christianity by the time it got consolidated in India.

On the other hand, the Hindu society throughout its long history, had neither displayed any sort of religious fanaticism, nor ever used the state power for spreading any faith. To preach Secularism to this society, was like showing a lamp to the sun. In such a country, Secularism could have relevance only in one sense — to establish complete cultural freedom in the Hindu homeland by eliminating the fanaticism which had survived in the form of Islam and Christianity.

This was a task of education. By confronting the Muslims and Christians with the close connection between their scriptures and their blood-soaked histories, it had to be explained to them that the teachings which they believed to be God-given were, in reality, expressions of beastliness latent in human nature. Of the ethos which the Hindu society has cherished as dharmic, not a trace can be found in Islam or Christianity. The right use of Secularism would have been to unmask these closed creeds and liberate the communities which had become their victims.

The Intellectual Perversion

But what happened in India after independence, was just the opposite. The mullahs and missionaries who had exhibited ceaseless hostility towards the ancient culture of this country, began to speak with one voice that there was a great danger to the religions and cultures of the Muslims and Christians from the majority Hindu society, and that the state would have to protect them by all means. It was, as the saying goes, उल्टा चोर कोतवाल को डाँटे (the thief accusing the policeman who had caught him red-handed). The Hindu society, in fact, had always suffered atrocities at the hands of the Muslims and Christians and never given even a threat of retaliation. But the party in power agreed with the mullahs and missionaries, and conceded many privileges to the so-called minorities in the Constitution of India. The Muslims and Christians were given complete freedom to propagate and spread their creeds to the best of their capacity. And this suicidal policy was advertised as 'secularism'.

The evil consequences of this pervert policy began to appear very soon. The Muslims, after obtaining support of the ruling party, began to spread their tentacles all around. By clamouring in the name of the distinctive culture of Islam and special rights of the minorities, they began to raise the same kind of demands because of which only some time back the country had been partitioned and rivers of blood had flown. And in support of these demands, they began to stage riots as well. At the same time, the Christian missionaries obtained unlimited funds from the Western countries and began to extend their network all over the country.

Some patriotic people could not remain mute spectators to all this. They came out against this perversion of Secularism. The ruling party issued a fatwa at once that the people pointing an accusing finger at Secularism were communalists and enemies of national unity. In due course, a new meaning of Secularism began to be fortified — Secularism, that is, applause for Islam and Christianity. And Hindu society began to be denounced as a nest of narrow-minded and aggressive communalism. The English-educated intelligentsia of this country in particular adopted these new formulations wholeheartedly. All political parties also began to swear by this Secularism.

The Christian missionaries had never had any shortage of money. The mullahs also began to receive unlimited funds from Arab countries due to exorbitant increase in the price of petrol in the eighth decade of this century. And because of the campaigns mounted by Islam and Christianity, the situation has now become quite frightful. Many people who supported Secularism till the other day, have now begun to admit that something has seriously gone wrong somewhere.

Scrutiny of the Perversion

Why did Secularism acquire this perverted form in India ? Why has the ideology of fanaticism to get rid of which Europe had developed Secularism, fattened in this country in the guise of Secularism ? The right answers to these vital questions have to be found by the Hindu society.

The story of sticking the stigma of communalism on the Hindu society, had started before India attained independence. The leaders of the Indian National Congress had tried to make the Muslims partners in the struggle for independence by extending many concessions to them. But the Muslims had never yielded to the Congress, and remained allies of British imperialism upto the end . The leaders of the Congress had never tried to understand this Muslim behaviour pattern. The more they failed to bring around the Muslims, the more they blamed their failure on the so-called Hindu communalism. In their opinion, it was Hindu communalism which, by inciting Muslim communalism, had become a stumbling block in their way. Thus the leaders of the Congress had confirmed the adage according to which when a potter cannot control the potteress, he twists the ears of his donkey.

In the last phase of the struggle for independence, a leftist faction had risen inside the Congress. The leader of this faction was Pandit Jawaharlal Nehru. Inspired by the Soviet Union and Communism, this faction had harboured a deep-seated animosity against Hindu society and culture. In the opinion of this faction, Islam was propagator of an equalitarian social system while the ancient culture of India stood for all sorts of inequalities and caste discriminations. The members of this faction had as much knowledge of Islam as that of Sanatana Dharma, that is, they were equally ignorant about both. They were only repeating the propaganda being promoted by the Communist Party of India which viewed the ancient culture of this country as its main enemy. But because of being powerful in the Congress, this faction succeeded to a great extent in blackening Hindu society and culture.

And when India became independent, this faction rose to power under Pandit Jawaharlal Nehru. History stands witness that the Muslims could divide the country only because they were patronized by this faction. But this faction passed the whole blame of partition on to the so-called Hindu communalism. Those people who fought for united India and had stubbornly resisted partition, were now being held responsible for partition by the ruling party! And it was for the sake of defaming these people that the new leaders of the Congress

Party raised the slogan of Secularism. Thus the policy of Secularism proclaimed by Pandit Nehru after attainment of independence, was, from the very beginning, full of animosity towards the Hindu society and culture. The consequences of this policy which followed in due course, should surprise no one.

The reason why Hindu society has remained incapable of defeating this policy, is that this society has got engaged in the self-destructive process of being on the defensive without understanding this perversion of Secularism. Whenever the enemies of this society accuse it of being communal, it starts breast-beating and wailing that this accusation is without substance. This society cannot muster the courage to proclaim that it is the national society of India, and that people who accuse it of being communal are themselves traitors to the nation, straight away.

A more serious mistake that Hindu society has committed is to keep on repeating the slogan of 'sarva-dharma-samabhāva' — equal regard for all dharmas — with regard to Islam and Christianity. The principle of sarva-dharma- samabhāva has always been accepted and practised among the schools of Sanatana Dharma. But to entertain samabhāva (equal regard) towards Islam and Christianity, by giving them the status of dharma, is to extend invitation to doom. A study of the scriptures, traditions and history of Islam and Christianity, makes it more than evident that these ideologies are not worthy of being called dharma in any sense of the term. Contrary to this, these ideologies are brimful of imperialistic ambitions. By accepting them as dharma, it becomes impossible to resist their imperialistic expansion. There should be no place for doubt in this matter. Wherever the impact of Islam and Christianity has grown, it has given fillip to treason. Afghanistan, Pakistan and Bangladesh were inseparable parts of India for ages past. Islam severed these parts from the motherland. In the North-East region of India, the increasing spell of Christianity is also inciting moves of separatism in the same way.

Treatment of the Disease

Therefore, if Hindu society wants to survive, it would have to proclaim loud and clear the following basic principles of Hindu culture:

1. The society which is known as Hindu society at present, is the national society of India.

2. Indian culture as nourished by the Sanatana Dharma and flourishing through many schools and sects, is the national culture of India.

3. The history of the Hindu society, is the history of India.

4. India is one indivisible whole.

The following conclusions which flow from these basic, principles, would also have to be accepted, acknowledged and proclaimed by the national society:

1. The imperialisms of Islam and Christianity have disappeared from this country, and, therefore, there remains no place in this country for Islam and Christianity.

2. The communities which have been crystallized in India as a result of the imperialistic expansion of Islam and Christianity, are our own people and will have to be brought back into the national society.

3. The national society is secular by its very nature and people who accuse it of being communal and practise hostility towards the ancient culture of India in the name of Secularism, are traitors, no matter how powerful, celebrated and self-satisfied these people may be at present.

4. The national society not only takes the pledge that, hereafter, it will not allow any community to divide India but also resolves that those parts of India which Islam has severed and those members of the national society whom Islam and Christianity have alienated from their ancestral culture, will be brought back to their national homeland and their national society.

This call can go forth from the national society only when its intelligentsia and its leaders acquire a full understanding of

Sanatana Dharma and its culture, and become committed to it with deep devotion. These conclusions can be drawn only when the intelligentsia of the national society and its leaders evaluate Islam and Christianity from the viewpoint of Sanatana Dharma, and understand the imperialistic and anti-humanistic character of these ideologies.

Chapter – 3

Challenge of Islam and Hindu Response

Islam had set its foot on the Hindu homeland in the second half of the seventh century. From then on till today, this creed has remained a nightmare for Hindu society and culture. Islam has victimised, tormented and terrorised the Hindu society in many ways. It has inflicted many wounds on Hindu culture. Some integral parts of India, have become foreign countries by falling into the clutches of Islamic imperialism. Many members of Hindu society have become self-alienated after having been terrorised or tempted by Islam. Today, the same people are behaving with deep animosity against Hindu society and culture.

In 1947, at the time of conceding partition, it had been proclaimed that the so-called communal problem had been solved for all time to come. But hardly fifty years have passed and the followers of Islam have again started speaking the same language which they had used before the partition of India. Communal riots have again started assuming terrible form. And the elements harbouring hostility towards the Hindu society, have again started cursing 'Hindu communalism'. The situation has deteriorated to such an extent that today a Hindu hesitates in making himself known as a Hindu. Being apologetic all the time, has become a habit of the Hindu society.

Why has all this happened, and is happening? The Hindu society will have to find an answer to this question. There should be no delay in this matter. Otherwise, this time the very survival of Hindu society will certainly become difficult, if not impossible, because the vast wealth that Islam has acquired through its stores of oil has once again rejuvenated and made it aggressive. A part of this wealth is being spent for creating many turmoils in this country, and will continue to do so more and more with increasing speed. If the need arises, the followers of Islam living in India will also easily obtain arms and ammunitions. At that time, the self-appointed custodians of Secularism will not be found anywhere on the scene. We should remember how these cowards ran away from Pakistan and Bangladesh, after having sung for years the glories of Islam and cursed 'Hindu communalism'. The storm will have to be faced by the Hindu society alone.

The Basic Blunder

After having studied Islamic scriptures and Islamic history as unfolded in my own country and abroad, I have reached the definite conclusion that Hindu society has committed a fundamental and suicidal blunder. It is because of this blunder that Hindu society has not been able to diagnose the epidemic till today. And if this blunder is not corrected, there will be no end to this epidemic.

That blunder is to recognize Islam as a dharma. How many more blunders have been committed and are being committed as a consequence of this basic blunder, is the subject-matter of this chapter. Discussion of this subject is being undertaken in the perspective of history.

Response in the First Phase

The founder of Islam, Muhammad, died in 632 (CE). After that event, within twenty years, a gangster horde raised by him in Arabia trampled under its feet all nations and cultures upto the western frontiers of India. Among those so utterly destroyed, the ancient and powerful Persian empire was the most prominent. But the same gangster horde had to struggle strenuously for seventy years before crossing the frontier of Sindh. The small Hindu states of Sindh, Sauvir and Gandhar put to flight again and again the armies sent repeatedly by the Caliphs at Damascus. All these accounts recorded by the contemporary and later Muslim historians, are readily available in history books. Thereafter, an Arab army penetrated into Sindh in 712 (CE), and by stages its raids reached Ujjain in the east, Kangra in the north, and Navasari towards the south. How that army was defeated by Hindu heroism and finally became besieged in Multan and Mansura — all this history has also been written by contemporary Muslim chroniclers. But nowhere do we find in history, indigenous or Islamic, even a hint as to what Hindu society thought of and surmised about Islam which had inspired these armies.

It cannot be said that Islam had left anything undone in making itself well known. Slaughter of the defeated armies after they had surrendered, public auction abroad of thousands of men and women and children who had been captured and sent there, mass rape of helpless women, destruction of temples, burning of the sacred books of dharma, breaking of idols of the gods, plunder of all kinds of property — all these doings of the Islamized Arabs have been applauded by the Muslim theologians and historians and proclaimed as the great triumph of Islam. At the same time, they have quoted those passages from the Quran and Hadis according to which to do all this is obligatory and meritorious in Islam.

But if the contemporary thinkers of Hindu society who saw or heard of all these atrocities drew any conclusions about the character of Islam, no clue is available anywhere in the contemporary indigenous literature. Internecine wars had often been fought in India. The Greek, Saka and Huna tribes had also mounted many invasions from outside India, descriptions of which are available from Indian sources. But the devil dance enacted by the armies of Islam, was wholly unprecedented for Hindu society. Slaughtering of people who had surrendered, capturing and exporting of innocent persons to foreign countries, dishonouring helpless women, plundering the defeated people — all these atrocities were unthinkable in the Indian tradition and history uptil then. And the most unthinkable of all was the fact that Islamic armies committed all these fiendish deeds by invoking verbatim their religious scriptures. Even so, the thinkers of India did not undertake any critical study of these unprecedented happenings. Accounts of the unequalled heroism which Hindu Rajas displayed in face of the Islamic armies, are available in contemporary and later Indian literature as also in inscriptions. But there is no allusion to any careful study of and contemplation on the gangster mentality of the these armies.

It cannot be said that India was bereft of thinkers in that period. The life-time of Adi Shankaracharya is considered contemporary to Arab invasions. A detailed description of many other contemporary thinkers — Buddhist, Jain, Vaishnava, Shaiva, Shakta, Tantrik, Yogic — is also available from those times. It is not conceivable that none of them had heard the name of Islam, or accounts of the atrocities committed by its armies. But all these thinkers could not entertain any proposition beyond ब्रह्म सत्यं जगन्मिथ्या (Brahma alone is Real, the world is an illusion). Perhaps evil conduct in this unreal world was no more than an illusion for them. Perhaps they could see no reason for discussing an illusion.

After being defeated in the very first adventure, the armies of Islam did not turn their face towards India for the next two hundred years. But some so-called saints of Islam came and settled down in many towns and villages, particularly in northern India and along the west coast. Muslim historians are witness as to how the Hindu Rajas and ordinary people welcomed these imposters, and how they were given land and money for building mosques and khanqahs. And when these charlatans began converting some Hindus to Islam, no one checked them. The sorcery, magic spells and 'miracles' performed by them, enchanted the minds of many Hindus. No one paid any attention to the fact that it were these very 'saints' had some time back applauded wholeheartedly the advancing Arab armies, and held the latter's atrocities wholly proper and sanctioned by Islam. Therefore, it is not a matter of surprise that at a later stage these Muslim 'saints', worked as spies for Islam in India, and guided Mahmud Ghaznavi to Nandana, Kangra, Thanesar, Mathura, Kannauj, Kalanjar and Somnath. Muslim historians do sing praises of the services rendered by Muslim saints in the advancement of Islam, and rightly so. But why do Hindus perform pilgrimages to the tombs of these despicable characters, offer homage to them with great devotion, and sing and listen to *qawwalis*? The only reason for this aberration has been that Hindu society has recognized Islam as a dharma.

Hindu society was never wanting in heroism. Mahmud Ghaznavi returned to Ghazni again and again after plundering and slaughtering, not because he did not want to annex India to his empire but because, leaving aside Punjab and some parts of Sindh, he could not conquer any other kingdom. The rising tide of the Hindu counter-attacks from all sides, had been forcing him every time to retrace his steps and return. It may be remembered that Ghaznavi was an incomparable military general of his time, and that he had expanded his empire far and wide in Khurasan and Iran.

But while Hindu society used armed prowess, it did not make use of the power of thought. In the abundant literature composed by the Hindu thinkers of that period, no indication is available that anyone had identified the essential character of Islam. Nor is there any indication that anyone censured the swindlers known as sufis on account of their questionable character. The Ghazi (*kāfir*-killer) of Islam (Mahmud) who had been invited by the sufis went back acknowledging defeat, but the sufi *silsilas* (orders) remained established, flourished, and continued getting funds and reverence from within India. In the *khanqahs* (monasteries) of these sufis, there were caged those helpless Hindu women who had been captured by Ghaznavi and presented to them as their reward. The sufis had also received an ample share of the Indian wealth plundered by Ghaznavi. They continued enjoying the wealth and the women in a mood of bliss. The wail of the helpless Hindu women did not bother Hindu society. On the contrary, simply because they had fallen into the hands of the *mlechhas* (unclean barbarians) those helpless women were damned as outside the pale.

This was the reason that, after another 150 years, Muhammad Ghauri marched against India raising once again the battle-cry of Islam. The sufi named Muinuddin Chishti who was later on buried in Ajmer, also accompanied him. In 1178 (CE), Ghauri fled after he was defeated near Abu by an army commanded by the widow queen of the Chaulukya king of Gujarat. In 1191, the same Ghauri fled again after he was beaten by Prithvi Raj Chauhan. At that time, the Chaulukya and Chauhan empires had so much power that, by pursuing Ghauri, they could have recaptured the north-western region seized by Islam and, after crushing Ghazni and Ghaur, stormed the Kabah wherefrom the Islamic epidemic had been spreading terror in India in wave after wave. It was the claim of Islam that the Hindu temples were built of brick and mortar, that Hindu idols of the gods were only pieces of stone, and that those temples and idols possessed no power of self-protection. This insane argument could have been countered only by the destruction of all mosques from Lahore to Mecca. Islam would have then realized at once that its Kabah also had no power of self-protection, that it was also made of brick and mortar, and that the piece of black stone enshrined in it was only a piece of stone. Hindu heroism went waste because the power of thought was not used to analyses the situation. Chishti entrenched himself at Ajmer, and sent word to Ghauri that victory over the Hindu armies could be won not by military might but by deception.

Ghauri followed Chishti's advice. In 1192 (CE), when he returned to the battlefield of Tarauri, the Chauhan King reminded him of how he had run away last time. Ghauri replied that he had come not on his own but on orders from his elder brother, Sultan Ghiyasuddin of Ghaur, and could not go back without obtaining orders from him. He also said that he had sent the message of Prithvi Raj to his elder brother, and that he would refrain from fighting till the latter's orders arrived. The Rajput army laid aside its arms, and that very night Ghauri's army defeated and dispersed it. But no Hindu took the trouble to know the fact that practising deception with the Kafirs was sanctioned by the scriptures of Islam. The Hindu literature of this period is full of the tales of Rajput heroism. But not a word is found there about the scriptures of Islam. As a result, Chishti remained established blissfully in Ajmer and continued exhibiting his 'miracles'. Witnessing the destruction of Hindu temples of Ajmer, Chishti offered thanks to his Allah. Allah had gained victory, and the face of infidelity had been blackened. No wonder, Allah made Ajmer the principal place of Islamic pilgrimage in India. The rice cooked, the flowers offered, and the wealth amassed at the tomb of Chishti, are partly the gifts from Hindus. But no Hindu till today has taken the trouble to know who really was the sufi entombed there, and how terrible was the traitorous role he had played against India. The reason, again, is that the Hindu society has accepted Islam as a dharma.

Response in the Second Phase

Ghauri laid the foundation of the rule of Islam in India. One of his army commanders, Bakhtiyar Khilji, attacked the Buddhist monasteries in Bihar, massacred Buddhist monks, burnt libraries of the universities situated there, and destroyed many Buddhist temples. After his conquest of Bengal, he was defeated in Assam and killed. Another army commander of Ghauri, Qutbuddin Aibak, erected the Quwwat-ul-Islam (Might of Islam) masjid at Delhi with the debris of 27 Hindu temples he had demolished and also destroyed the remaining temples in Ajmer. Thereafter, all succeeding sultans committed detestable deeds of similar nature, wherever they could.

The idols from the temples were placed under the stairs of mosques and as footsteps in the lavatories of sultans and amirs. Most of the historical masjids and khanqahs found in India today, have been built by destroying Hindu temples and monasteries or after desecrating them. The Archaeological Survey of India has copious records of this holocaust. Besides this, many other atrocities — rape of helpless women, dishonouring and killing of sadhus and saints, cold-blooded slaughter of people defeated in war including the young and the aged, capture and sale of Hindu men and women and children as slaves, plunder of Hindu properties, killing of cows, humiliation of Brahmins by shaving their heads and breaking their sacred threads — were heaped on Hindus nonstop. Mamluk, Khilji, Tughlaq, Sayyad, Lodi — in the reigns of all the rulers of these Muslim dynasties, from the beginning of the thirteenth century to the end of the fifteenth, this process continued.

Islamic law has four schools — Hanbali, Maliki, Shafii and Hanafi. The first three schools advocated that the Hindus were not People of the Book, like the Christians and the Jews, that is, they did not possess any revealed scriptures such as the Old Testament of the Jews, the New Testament of the Christians and the Quran of the Muslims — the three Books revealed by the same 'God' to these peoples through his prophets sent form time to time. Therefore, according to these three schools, the Hindus had either to convert and become Muslims, or had to be killed. They could not be treated as Zimmis (protected subjects), and spared their lives by paying Jizyah (poll-tax) as well as submitting to disabilities imposed on them. Only the Hanafi school held that the Hindus could also be accepted as People of the Book and made Zimmis. The sultans and the Muslim army commanders spared no efforts to see that Hindus became Muslims, or were wiped out. But Hindu heroism had not been exhausted. They kept on ceaseless resistance. In the end, the sultans and the army commanders became weary of waging wars. They accepted defeat and proclaimed that, in

India, Islam was adherent of the Hanafi school of law. Hearing this proclamation, the sufis and the ulema got very much perturbed. But the sufis and the ulema did not have to fight in the fields. The sultans simply ignored them.

One of these sufis was Nizamuddin Auliya whose tomb in Delhi continues to be revered by the Hindus. His principal disciple was Amir Khusrau on whom honours are heaped even today by many Hindus. Khusrau was a court poet, and writing eulogies of the ruling sultan was his only profession. Soon after writing the eulogy of one sultan, he would write a similar one for another who ascended the throne by murdering the earlier one. The extension of the Hanafi law to the Hindus, made him feel greatly enraged. He wrote: "The heroism of our holy warriors has saturated the whole country with streams (of blood) flowing from the sword (of Islam). The clouds of infidelity have been dispersed. The mighty warriors of Hind have been trampled under foot. Now they are all ready to become tax-payers. Islam has triumphed and the head of infidelity has been laid low. If the Hanafi code of law had not saved the Hindus from death by levying Jizyah, they would have been annihilated root and branch."

Hindus continued fighting with steadfastness against the Jihad of Islam. In the South, the two great Hindu warriors who had been converted to Islam — Harihar and Bukka — were brought back into the fold of Hinduism by Acharya Madhavaranya and they established the Vijayanagara Empire. It was under the protection of that Empire that Hindu Shastras were revived and Sayana's commentaries on the Vedas were composed. That Empire halted the storm of Islam for 250 years from advancing further south. But no captain or thinker of that Empire tried to study Islam. Consequently, the number of Muslims went on increasing continuously in the army of the Empire, and it was the treachery practised by them in a decisive battle which destroyed that Empire.

It cannot be said that the rulers and thinkers of Vijayanagara, had no knowledge of the criminal character of Islam. The queen of a prince of Vijayanagara, Ganga Devi, had composed an epic named *Madhurā Vijayam* at the end of the fourteenth century (CE). The atrocities that had been committed by the Muslims during their rule in Madhura (modern Madurai), are described by her as follows: "Those vicious barbarians (*mlechhas*) mount attacks on the Hindu Dharma every day. They break the idols of the gods and throw away the vessels of worship. They cast into fire the *Srimadbhāgavata* and the other *dharmagranthas* (dharmic books), lick away the sandal paste from the bodies of the Brahmins, urinate on the Tulasi plants like dogs, deliberately defecate in the temples, gargle over the Hindus engaged in worship, and terrorise Hindu saints. It appears as if all these people have escaped from some lunatic asylum."

No thinker of Vijayanagara tried to search for the source of this Muslim insanity. No one tried to know that in the scriptures of Islam, gangsters of this type have not been censured as mad but hailed as Ghazis (great heroes). If some Hindu thinker had studied the scriptures of Islam and perceived the behaviour pattern prescribed in them, he would have warned his society that the Hindus had to deal not with mad people but with gangsters fanaticized by Islam. Thereafter, the Hindu society would have perhaps discovered the remedy for this fanaticism.

In the scriptures of Islam, it is clearly stated that Islam is the only and the final truth, and that anyone raising any sort of doubt as regards that truth should be killed immediately. In this situation, to say that the Hindu Dharma also had some truth in it was a cardinal crime. Even so, Kabir, Nanak and some other Hindu saints committed this 'crime'. They said it again and again that the Hindu Dharma was as good for the Hindus as Islam was for the Muslims, and that the attainment that was possible through Islam was possible through the Hindu Dharma also. Now-a-days some people say that Kabir and Nanak, by proclaiming Islam as a dharma, were the first to spread that falsehood which later on proved disastrous. There is some substance in this allegation. But viewing it in the context of that period, it has to be admitted that this comparing of the Hindu Dharma with Islam and describing the Hindu Dharma as equal to Islam, was an act of great courage. Kabir had to suffer many torments at the hands of Sikandar Lodi for coming out with that sort of courage. Guru Nanak escaped this treatment because, in his period of preaching, the Muslim empire in India was once again in decline and the attention of some subedar of Lahore or the sultan of Delhi was not drawn towards him.

This indeed was the foremost achievement of the Hindu response to the challenge of Islam, which was witnessed in the second phase of Muslim imperialism. As a result of Hindu heroism, Muslim rule had not been able to become firmly established. Now-a-days, a detailed description of a few medieval Muslim empires is found in the textbooks of history. But on taking a count of the duration of these 'empires', it becomes clear that, leaving aside the Mughal empire, no Muslim regime could stay in power for more than 20-30 years. It was all due to repeated revolts staged by the Hindu Rajas and the people in general, and their display of heroism. When Babur invaded India, the most powerful kingdoms in the country were those of Mewar and Vijayanagar. No sultan had the capacity to wage war against Maharana Sanga and Krishnadeva Raya. The Lodi 'emperor' at Agra had absolutely none.

It this period, besides Hindu heroism, another development also took place. The Hindu society stood together in spurning the Muslims as untouchables. Most of the Muslims in India were those who had been forcibly dragged or allured into the fold of Islam from within the Hindu society. Many a time, it had also happened that some families from a particular Hindu caste became Muslims for some reason while the others continued to remain Hindus. But far from sharing food or entering into marriage relations, Hindus and Muslims of the same caste did not share even drinking water. To shun even the shadow of a Muslim by regarding him an untouchable, may be a controversial subject in the democratic and social-istic age of today. But a society, caught in the clutches of calamity, has to save itself in this manner, especially a society the thought power of which has declined and which is engaged in building its defences by relying on its ancestral traditions.

It has to be admitted that sometimes the achievement of one age becomes a liability in another age. And that is what happened in this case. The trend of accepting Islam as a dharma, which some Hindu saints had initiated in an earlier age, proved to be a very great hurdle in the following age. Similarly, by regarding every Muslim as untouchable, the Hindu society closed its doors for ever on those of its members who had been alienated from it by force or allurement. If Islam had been identified ideologically by means of study and intellectual analysis, the heroism and tenacity for tradition displayed one day would not have boomeranged another day.

Response in the Third Phase

The display of heroism by the Hindu nation succeeded in the long run. By the time of Akbar, the Muslim invaders came to understand that Hindus by and large could neither be made Muslims by force nor suppressed for long. Consequently, Akbar arrived at a compromise with the Hindus, and made the Rajputs partners in the expansion of his empire. The Mughal empire gained much by this policy. But the Hindu nation also gained no less. Akbar had rejected the system of administra-tion ordained by Islam. Cow slaughter was banned. Jiziyah, the tax payable by the Hindus to a Muslim ruler for protection of life and property, was abolished. Hindus could now visit their holy places without paying pilgrim tax. A Hindu male could now marry a Muslim female without becoming Muslim. Hindus also got the freedom to criticize Islam, and they could point a finger even at the conduct of the prophet of Islam if they wished. At the same time, any Hindu converted to Islam obtained the right to return back to the Hindu society.

But the Hindus did not care to take advantage of this good opportunity. Neither the Hindus married Muslim women, nor the Hindus converted to Islam returned back to the Hindu society. No indication is available from that period that any Hindu studied or made any critical comments on Islam. What happened was only this much that the Hindu society heaved a sigh of relief after ceaseless strife for several hundred years.

On the other hand, the insistence of Hindu saints that the Hindu Dharma is rich in all respects began to have some effect. During Akbar's rule, Hindu Shastras came to be studied by some Muslims. It was but natural that Muslim scholars determined the substance of the Hindu Dharma by weighing it on the scales of Islam. And that is what happened too. Monotheism and prophets were searched in the Hindu Shastras. Obviously, this was not the proper method to understand the Hindu Dharma. This meant that the Hindu Dharma was being cast in the mould of Islam. But the fact that some Muslims could do even this much during the days of their dominance, was not a small thing. Muslims like Rahim and Raskhan went even further.

But there is such a dense darkness in the core of Islam that even a single ray of light dazzles it. Having once closed its eyes towards rationality and decent behaviour befitting human beings, it could never open them again. After witnessing what happened during Akbar's rule, the sufis and the ulema raised an alarm. And during the time of Shah Jahan's rule, the grip of Islam began to be tightened once again on the system of government. Aurangzeb reversed the policy of Akbar cent per cent. Once again, the Hindu was left with no option except war and heroism.

The rise of Samarth Ramadas took place in this period. In this very period, Shivaji, the man who shaped the age, also took birth. The Rajput sword was unsheathed in Rajasthan, and the Sikh sword in the Punjab. All around Delhi, the Jats displayed great heroism. The Bundelas rose up in the vales of Vindhyachal. Aurangzeb could not overcome this storm. By the time he neared his death, he felt completely defeated. The armies of the Marathas had started challenging Mughal authority in Gujrat and Malwa during the last days of his rule.

Hardly fifty years had passed after the death of Aurangzeb, when Muslim rule in India drew towards its end. Now the Marathas were the mightiest power in India. The Mughal 'emperor' at Delhi was dependent on their mercy. But for want of the power of thought, the Hindus lost the game once again. The Marathas did not wipe out Islam when they had the opportunity. The power of Islam at this time was centred in the hands of those few whose ancestors had come into India as foreign invaders or as their servitors. These people called themselves Arabs, Turks, Mughals, Iranians etc., and looked down upon the common Muslims who were converts from the Hindu society. The need of the time was that the Hindu society threw open its doors to the native converts, and either expelled the foreign Muslims from India or pulled out their fangs full of the poison of Islam. But what happened was the exact opposite. The Marathas and Sikhs tried to make friends with the foreign Nawabs and Amirs descended from Muslim invaders, and disregarded the native converts to Islam. It was proved in the Third Battle of Panipat as to who was with whom. But by then, the opportune time had passed. The foreign Muslims first sought the help of Ahmad Shah Abdali and, thereafter, took shelter under the British. Even now, Hindu society, was sitting tight with its doors closed on the native Muslims. At the same time, this society did not tire of proclaiming that Islam was as great a dharma as the Hindu Dharma.

The British invasion progressed in India and, after the Great Rebellion of 1857, it settled down firmly. The propagation of this lie is very widespread that the leaders of the Rebellion were Muslims. The British themselves had spread this lie. It is true that, among the leaders of the Rebellion, there were some Muslim Nawabs, particularly in the region known as Uttar Pradesh today. But the British themselves had made a count of the soldiers who had displayed heroism during the Rebellion. Their statistics tell us that, among those soldiers, the number of Hindus was many times more than that of the Muslims. Among the leaders of the Rebellion also, the valour of Tantia Tope, Rani Lakshmi Bai, and Kunwar Singh, exceeded by far the exploits of any Muslim Nawab. Hindu leaders, however, kept on invoking the name of the Mughal 'emperor'. On the other hand, the Muslims also convinced themselves that the British had grabbed power to rule India from the Muslim empire. If the Marathas had unfurled the saffron flag over Delhi in due time by kicking away the Mughal skeleton, this lie would not have gained any support at a later stage.

This lie bore fruit in the last quarter of the nineteenth century, when the freedom movement against British imperialism took birth. Prior to this, many waves of social reforms and cultural awakening had surged forward in Hindu society. The founder of the Arya Samaj, Maharshi Dayananda, had proclaimed that Islam was no dharma but only a subterfuge of blind beliefs. Having witnessed this new and brightened face of the Hindu nation, the remnants of Muslim imperialism, that is, the foreign Muslims, were already perturbed. Now, on hearing another tune from the same nation, they became terribly frightened. These remnants of Muslim imperialism were flourishing under the protection of British imperialism. Suddenly, they raised a hue and cry and began to bewail, "The Muslim nation which was the ruling race till yesterday, cannot accept a status of equality with the Hindu nation which was in attendance on the Muslims till the other day." At the same time, these remnants began to hurl threats that the Muslim race also knew how to wield the sword, which the Hindu Banias were incapable of doing. But a close look at this self-adulation, revealed how terribly frightened these remnants of Muslim imperialism were. That was why they were praying with one voice that the white masters should not introduce any democratic institutions in India, and never leave the land.

The need of the time was that the freedom struggle which

the leaders of the country were waging, should have had a two-pronged strategy. The freedom movement had to battle not only against British imperialism, but also against the remnants of Muslim imperialism. The struggle against Muslim imperialism had been going on since the thirteenth century (CE). The Vijayanagara Empire, Rana Sanga and Maharana Pratap had made great contributions to that long-drawn-out war. Its tide had been turned by the diplomatic as well as the military skill of Chhatrapati Shivaji. This struggle had remained unfinished because of the intervention of British imperialism. Now that old struggle had to be resumed and led to its successful conclusion. But this was not done, and Islam became a problem for the country once again. The only reason for this sorry outcome was that, by accepting Islam as a dharma, the Muslims had been given the status of a religious minority.

In the Swadeshi Movement which surged forward after the partition of Bengal, the battle being fought against the British had been linked with the battles fought earlier against Muslim imperialism. But only for a brief period. The proclamation of Maharshi Dayananda that Islam was no dharma, was also re-echoed at some places for some days. But not with self-confidence. Consequently, the suffocation which pervaded the political and cultural atmosphere, could not be cleared. On the other hand, having witnessed the rising tempo of the freedom movement, Muslim leaders hatched a conspiracy to use the movement for serving the interests of Pan-Islamism and extended their hand for cooperation against the British rule. The leaders of the nation became convinced that the mentality of the Muslims had changed, and that the traitors of yesterday had become patriots of today. Hence, in 1916, the Lucknow Pact was signed by Lokamanya Tilak on behalf of the Indian National Congress. The Pact conceded all the communal demands that had been made by the Muslim leader till then. The way Islam rode on the back of the freedom movement during the Khilafat movement was a clear indication that the leaders of the nation had not understood the real character of Islam, and, consequently, would not be able to defeat the designs of Islam. Some thinkers like Sri Aurobindo, Sarat Chandra Chatterji and Lala Lajpat Rai, had issued a warning that the strategy of the freedom movement be formulated after a proper study of Islam. Veer Savarkar and Dr. Hedgewar had come forward to defeat the designs of Islam. But Gandhi's slogan of *sarva-dharma-samabhāva*, had sent the country into a deep slumber. Once again, the Muslims co-operated with the British imperialism. All the sacrifices in the freedom movement were made by the Hindu society, but by staging streets riots from time to time and by issuing threats of widespread bloodshed, Islam partitioned the country. If it had been understood in due time that Islam was no dharma but only a political doctrine of imperialism, it might have saved the country from the frightful outcome.

Response in the Fourth Phase

After partition, independent India resolved to follow four basic policies — democracy, socialism, secularism or *sarva-dharma-samabhāva*, and non-alignment. In principle, all the four policies were unobjectionable. But the remnants of Muslim imperialism in India, perverted the meaning of all four. Being irked by that perversion, some people have started opposing these policies in principle.

Some of the remnants of Muslim imperialism migrated to Pakistan after independence. But a section of them stayed in India and began to look for a new opportunity. A majority of this section joined the ruling Congress Party, and started utilising their positions for the service of Islam. Some of them joined the Communist Party, and began to advance the designs of Islam behind the smoke-screen of progressivism. And the rest, who entered various other political parties, began to get their support for Islamic causes. Party may be any, the goal to be achieved was the same — to secure the victory of Islam over the remaining part of India as well. The old Muslim organisations — Jamaat-i-Islami, Muslim League, Ittihad-ul-Musalmin, Jamiat-ul-Ulema-i-Hind — continued functioning as before.

The only difference that came about was that those people who, before partition, had proclaimed, with great pride and red-shot eyes, the Muslims as a separate nation in the name of religion, history and culture and threatened largescale bloodshed in order to have their way, now started raising cries of distress that the new policies of India were not being implemented in right earnest. It was the same old theme. Only the manner of presenting it had changed.

Invoking democracy, these people began to ask as to what sort of democracy was this in which a large section of the people (Muslims) did not get due representation in parliamentary institutions, government administration, the armed forces, and the police, etc.

Invoking socialism, these people began to ask as to what sort of socialism was this in which all the means of production and distribution were in the hands of the high caste Hindus, and in which the poor Muslims — destitute, downtrodden and exploited in every way — did not get sufficient food to fill their bellies and clothes to cover their bodies?

Invoking the policy of secularism or *sarva-dharma-samabhāva*, these people began to ask as to what sort of secularism was this in which all the government institutions and the media continued spreading the Hindu religion and culture, and the foremost champions of which went on pilgrimage to Hindu temples? And what sort of *sarva-dharma-samabhāva* was this in which the Muslim religion and culture got no protection, and in which a leading language like Urdu was neglected?

Invoking the policy of non-alignment, these people began to ask as to what sort of non-alignment was this in which the sentiments of a large section of the nation were ignored and the imperialistic aggression of Israel against the Arab nations was not opposed, and in which the interests of international Islam and of the Muslim nations found no place?

If someone pointed out to these invokers of democracy, socialism and secularism that they should also criticize those Muslim countries where not even the slightest trace of these policies could be detected, then all the Muslim leaders started shouting with one voice — What have we got to do with those foreign countries? We are only talking of India and of the policies adopted by India. If someone pointed out that if you really have nothing to do with foreign countries, then why do you feel concerned about happenings in the Muslim countries or with the policies pursued by the other nations towards them, why do you go on holding meetings and taking out processions and pressurising the government of India for supporting the Muslim nations, why do you stage street riots against the Hindus whenever something distasteful to you happens in some Muslim country or the other?, then all the Muslim leaders began to shout with one voice — all the Muslims of the world are indivisible parts of the one *millat* (Muslim fraternity), and Islam does not accept that any Muslim is only the citizen of the country where he resides.

If someone pointed out that you invoke secularism or *sarva- dharma-samabhāva* but in the scriptures of Islam, there is no place at all for secularism or any religion other than Islam, then all the Muslim leaders began to shout with one voice — you are the followers of secularism or *sarva-dharma-samabhāva*, not we; Islam does not allow entertainment of any such principle; therefore, this principle is not applicable to us; but, because you proclaim this principle, you cannot make any critical comment on Islam.

The vote-hungry political parties either kept quiet or agreed with the Muslim leaders. The Communists had equipped the Muslims with a weapon even before partition — whoever says that the demands of the Muslims are improper, or holds their complaints baseless, or raises a critical voice about Islam, or talks of protection for the Hindu dharma, culture and society, is a narrow-minded communalist with a fascist bent, a reactionary and blood-thirsty demon. The Muslims kept on using this weapon after partition also. The influence of the

Communist ideology had had a deep impact on the ruling Congress Party right from the time of Pandit Nehru's supremacy. That Party also echoed the howl of the Communists and Muslims. And, gradually, all political parties became panic-stricken lest the Muslims get offended and issue a fatwa against them. A competition started among political parties for displaying the Muslims who were party members, the prominent party posts that the Muslims held, the number of Muslim candidates who were given tickets at the time of elections, and the demands of the Muslims that were included in the election manifesto.

This process was in progress when the wailing Muslims suddenly began to roar. The Muslim countries in the Middle East had decided to test their oil reserves as a political weapon. The blow of that weapon was felt by all nations for some time. But all the others recovered before long. Only India reeled under that blow. Many international Muslim organisations began to proclaim that the destiny of Islam had taken a turn due to the blessings of Allah, and that the unfinished task of Islam in India must be finished. At the same time, fabulous funds began to be made available to the Muslims of India by the oil-rich Muslim countries. It need not be detailed here as to the uses being made of that money. Only those people have failed to see or hear or understand the current Islamic agenda in India who, because of their Communist or some other traitorous vision, harbour an anti-Hindu animus.

But this time a new response is coming forth from the Hindu society. A section of the Hindu intelligentsia and some Hindu organisations have not only drawn the attention of the Hindu society towards this new challenge of Islam, but also proclaimed that this aggression of Islam shall not be allowed to continue any longer. There are ample proofs that the new response is drawing attention of the Hindus at large. The Hindu society is now ready to hear that Islam is not a dharma but a totalitarian and imperialistic dogma which, by misusing the language of religion, throws dust in the eyes of others. This new voice of the nation has not yet become loud and clear; the leaders of the nation are still speaking in a subdued voice. But it can now be hoped that the day is not far off when the Hindu society will declare firmly that the imperialistic rule of Islam has disappeared, and that now there is no place for Islam in this country. That day will be the beginning of a Great Yajna which will stand completed only when all parts of the Hindu homeland occupied by Islam and all members of the Hindu society alienated from it by that ideology, will rejoin the motherland and the national mainstream. (See Appendices 1 and 2 for the national vision that is emerging.)

Appendix – 1

The Emerging National Vision

Speech delivered by Sita Ram Goel on Sunday the 4th December, 1983, at the Yogakshema monthly meeting at Calcutta.

Dr. Dhar, Mr. Ghosh and Friends,*

What Mr. Ghosh has said about me has added to my diffidence which was there from the very beginning because I am not used to public speaking. I do not know if I am a good writer at all. But I know it for sure that I am a very poor speaker. You will, therefore, forgive me if I am somewhat slipshod, if I become abrupt and incoherent at times.

In fact, it would have been in the fitness of things if the speaker today had been our friend Sri Ram Swarup, because whatever I have written and whatever I have to say today really comes from him. He gives me the seed-ideas which sprout into my articles, long and short. He gives me the perspective. He gives me the framework of my thought. Only the language is mine. The language also would have been much better if it was his own. My language becomes sharp at times; it annoys people. He has a way of saying things in a firm but polite manner, which discipline I have never been able to acquire. I wonder if he will be able to add some comments at the end of this meeting.

---

* Dr. Sujit Dhar and Shri Amitav Ghosh.

Now, coming to the subject of today, that is, the Emerging National Vision, I feel that perhaps it is presumptuous on my part to speak about the National Vision before an audience from Bengal, particularly before an audience from this city of Calcutta. It was in this land of Bengal, it was in this city of Calcutta in the opening decades of this century that we obtained a clear picture of the National Vision. You have only to read the works of Bankim Chandra, Vivekananda and Sri Aurobindo and listen to the songs of Rabindranath in order to know what that National Vision was, as also to understand what that Vision is likely to be when it revives and is reaffirmed. I have nothing to add to what these great men have written and expounded and what they have shown in their own lives. I am only a poor interpreter of their Vision as it should unfold, as it should emerge in the present situation.

The National Vision which was expounded by these great men rose to its heights, reached a high watermark, attained its acme in the Swadeshi Movement. The same imperialist forces, that is, Islamic imperialism (or the residues of Islamic imperialism) and British imperialism, had combined to partition Bengal, to partition a land which God had made one. But at that time, the conspiracy was frustrated. The game was defeated because the National Vision was very clear, very firm. In fact, the Swadeshi Movement was the beginning in real earnest of the National Struggle for Freedom which was earlier confined to some distinguished people meeting together and passing a number of resolutions. It was for the first time that India witnessed in the history of the freedom movement a mass mobilization of her people. The echoes of the Swadeshi Movement were heard far and wide, all over India, particularly in Maharashtra and the Punjab, as also the *mantras* that were given during the Swadeshi Movement — the *mantra* of Swadeshi, the *mantra* of Swarajya, the *mantra* of Vande Mataram which pulsated with all the aspirations of an awakened nation. That was a complete picture of the National Vision as it had to be.

But, unfortunately, in the hands of the latter-day leadership, in the later phases of the freedom struggle, that Vision got diluted. It was obscured by certain other visions. It lost its clarity and the result was the tragedy of partition. We know what happened and how the events unfolded. Bengal has suffered the most due to that tragedy. The wounds which Bengal has suffered and which have now become running sores — well, I do not have to dwell on the subject. You know it all. I have only to point out, it is my painful duty to point out, that this land of Bengal which has suffered so much due to the loss of the National Vision, has neglected that Vision to a greater extent than the rest of this country. It is, therefore, the duty of Bengal to resurrect that Vision, to recover that Vision, to reaffirm that Vision, and thus reclaim its lost leadership of India.

Bengal today feels neglected. But the fault is not of the rest of India. The fault lies with Bengal itself. Bengal has neglected its own heritage. Bengal has ignored its own Vision which it had once given to the whole of India and which, in turn, had given to Bengal the leadership of India. I need not go into details. You know what is happening in Bengal today. It is not only the perspective but also the personal character of its great men which is being questioned. As I read the various debates going on in the Bengali press, in Bengali novels and other writings, I am really pained. How can things go down to such a low level in a land which had once raised India to such great heights?

What was that National Vision which these great men gave us and which inspired India to launch such a great struggle for freedom? Remember the revolutionaries which India produced at that time. They were great men and women, those revolutionaries who mounted the gallows with the Gita in hand and with Vande Mataram on their lips. They were not like the latter-day revolutionaries. I can say with a full sense of responsibility that quite a few of the latter-day revolutionaries sound like ordinary criminals. The earlier revolutionaries were of a different character because their Vision was of a different character.

What was that Vision? In a way, it was nothing new. It was only a restatement in modern language, in a modern setting, of the ancient Vedic Vision as unfolded in the Vedas, in the Upanishads, in the Jainagama, in the Tripitaka, in the Ramayana and the Mahabharata, in the Puranas, in the Dharmashastras, and in the latter-day poetry of saints and siddhas. We have had countless spokesmen of that Vision throughout our history.

The first dimension of that Vision was that India was the land of Sanatana Dharma. That was the first and foremost point of that Vision. In fact, Sri Aurobindo had said in his Uttarpara Speech that India would rise with the rise of Sanatana Dharma, that India would sink if Sanatana Dharma sank, and that India would die if it were at all possible for Sanatana Dharma to die. This is not the occasion for me to talk about Sanatana Dharma. All I want to say is that Sanatana Dharma is a natural religion, that it is in harmony with the development of human nature, with the growth of human aspirations. It is not something artificial like Christianity and Islam. It is not a set of mechanical beliefs constructed by the outer mind of man and imposed upon its followers.

The second dimension of that Vision was that of a vast and variegated culture. According to *ādhāra* and *adhikāra*, the various sections of our population, various segments of our society, various regions of our country, developed their own culture, developed their own art, developed their own literature. We have a vast literature — sacred, secular and scientific — which grew in different regions of this country, in different social and cultural surroundings. We have a lot of art and literature. But its spirit is the spirit of Sanatana Dharma. It is informed by Sanatana Dharma in all its details. That was the second dimension of that National Vision.

The third dimension of that Vision was that this great society, the society which we describe as Hindu society today, was reared on the basis of spirituality, on the basis of Sanatana Dharma, on the basis of a great culture created by Sanatana Dharma. The Varnashrama Dharma which has shaped this great society has been corrupted today into a single English phrase — the Caste System which everybody is busy accusing of all sorts of crimes. But it was Varnashrama Dharma which created a complex social system that has survived till today with vitality and vigour, in spite of all vicissitudes of fortune, in spite of so many foreign invasions, throughout these countless ages. Varnashrama Dharma has been defended by all our great men in recent times. It was defended by Swami Dayananda, it was defended by Bankim Chandra, it was defended by Vivekananda, it was defended by Mahatma Gandhi, by Madan Mohan Malaviya, by Lokamanya Tilak. All these great men have been unanimous that Varnashrama Dharma has saved Hindu society from destruction — the destruction which overtook so many societies outside India at the hands of Christianity, Islam and Communism. That was the third dimension of that National Vision.

The fourth dimension of that National Vision was that this great society, this Hindu society, had a history of its own — a history of how this society arose, how it developed, how it created a spirituality which was akin to the spirituality of many ancient nations like Greece, Rome, China, Egypt, Persia. We were told that the history of India was the history of Hindu society, of Hindu culture, of Hindu spirituality, that it was the history of the Hindu nation and not the history of foreign invaders as we are being taught today. That was the fourth dimension of that National Vision.

And the last dimension which these great men stressed, which they affirmed again and again, was that this land of Bharatavarsha was one indivisible whole; that it was the cradle of Hindu society, of Hindu culture, of Hindu spirituality; that it was the homeland of the Hindu nation; and that other communities were welcome to live in this land provided they came to terms with Hindu society and Hindu culture. They did not think in terms of Afghanistan, Pakistan, Hindustan and Bangladesh. Today Bharatavarsha stands divided into several units which are not only politically but also culturally hostile to each other and we seem to have become reconciled to that division. But the Vision that was given to us by our great men was that of Bharatavarsha as an indivisible whole, not only geographically but also culturally. That Vision rose before us during the Swadeshi Movement, in the first decade of this century.

There were some other visions also, struggling for supremacy at the same time. Those other visions had an advantage on their side because of the educational system provided by the British, imposed on us by the British. This was the same educational system which we have in this country today. This educational system has been sponsoring and spreading those other visions of India.

There was the vision of Islamic imperialism. It said that India like pre-Islamic Arabia and pre-Islamic Persia and like so many other ancient lands conquered by Islam, was a land of darkness. It said that India had to be brought to the "light" of Islam, converted into a *dār al-Islam*.

Later on, another vision was provided by Christian imperialism. It also said that India was a land of darkness, of heathenism, of paganism, of unbelievers. It said that the "light" of Christianity had to be brought to India, that India had to be converted into a land of Christ.

A third vision came to us in the shape of the White man's burden. This vision shared somethings of the crusading zeal of Islamic and Christian imperialism. But it spoke in the language of rationalism and humanism. It spoke in an enlightened language. It said that India was a land of poor, illiterate, downtrodden, exploited and emasculated human beings who had to be given bread, who had to be educated, who had to be given health, who had to be given some sort of self-confidence by the British mentors or by Western culture imported from this foreign country or that.

Later still, another imperialist vision came from the West in the shape of Communism. This vision said that India was a colonial and semi-colonial society, divided into exploiting and exploited classes, into the oppressors and the oppressed, and that it was the duty of the Communist Party to liberate India from all this sloth and exploitation, this deadening of the forces of production. This was the fourth imperialist vision of India.

The cumulative effect of all these imperialist visions combining together has been rather serious, rather disastrous for us. Today the vision that prevails, particularly amongst our ruling classes, amongst the Hindu intellectuals, amongst the Hindu elite, is quite the opposite of the National Vision provided by the Swadeshi Movement, provided by our own great men.

Today we are told that Bharatavarsha is not one indivisible whole, that it is not one country. We are told that India is a subcontinent and that its division that has taken place into Afghanistan, Pakistan, Hindustan and Bangladesh is the natural outcome of various nationalities struggling for their own pieces of homeland. As a result, India can no more be claimed as its own homeland by any particular society, least of all by the Hindu society.

Then we are told that the history of this subcontinent is not the history of Hindu society, of the Hindu nation. This country is now regarded as some sort of a *dharmashālā* into which all sorts of invaders have poured in from the West and the East and other directions. The history of India has become the history of foreign invaders. So when you look at the teaching of history in our universities, colleges and schools, you find that there is an ancient Hindu period, you find that there is a medieval Muslim period, and you find that there is a modern British period. Now we are also informed of a contemporary period, the post-independence period, with its own architect and father.

Next we are told that Indian society is not a homogenous

society. India, we are told, is multi-racial, multinational, multi-linguistic and multi many other things. We are also told that Indian culture is not Hindu culture, that it is a composite culture made out of many cultures, indigenous and imported. It makes me laugh sometimes. When we talk of Indian music, we find that it is Hindu music. When we talk of Indian sculpture, we find that it is Hindu sculpture. When we talk of Indian architecture, we find that it is Hindu architecture except for a few minor details added by foreign invaders. Indian literature, almost ninety-nine percent of it, is Hindu literature. All this is Hindu heritage. It was the Hindus who created it, it is the Hindus who have sustained it. It is the Hindus who are still adding to it, elaborating it and expanding it. Yet, when it is pointed out that the culture of this country is Hindu culture and that the history of this culture is Hindus history, everyone seems to get annoyed. People who talk of Hindu culture are accused of being communalists.

But the strangest thing that has happened is that the religion of this country is no more Sanatana Dharma. Sanatana Dharma is now supposed to be some sort of a primitive superstition. Some people take up Vedanta and talk a lot about it. Some others take up the Gita and talk about the Gita. Some others take up and talk about other aspects of Sanatana Dharma, Yoga and so on. They acquire name and fame, write books and give lectures. But when it is pointed out that it was Sanatana Dharma which created all this spirituality, all this philosophy, all these laws, all this culture, not many people are prepared to accept it. A new religion has taken the place of Sanatana Dharma. This new religion is Secularism.

We are now told that it will be through Secularism that India will become a united nation, that there will be national integration on the basis of Secularism. So we have a National Integration Council. It gives instructions to the Ministry of Education that the history of India should be rewritten so that Muslim invaders of this country are not regarded as foreigners, so that Islamic imperialism is not regarded as something obnoxious, as something foreign, as something which came from outside. We are now required to accept Islam as an Indian religion, as a religion which must have as much pride of place in India as her own Sanatana Dharma. The logic has not yet been extended to the so-called British period of our history. But tomorrow there may be voices which demand that the British should not be regarded as invaders and injurers because, after all, they gave us English education, English literature, hospitals, schools, colleges, roads and all sorts of modern paraphernalia.

This is the state of things that is now prevailing in this country. The National Vision which had arisen during the Swadeshi Movement, which had mobilized the masses in India and which had taken her ahead in the fight for freedom, is now more or less completely eclipsed. It is not so much eclipsed elsewhere in India as in Bengal or in Kerala or in certain other parts where English education has spread faster than in other places. This is the situation that obtains today.

Let us take Secularism. It is a concept which we have imported from modern Europe. The Christian Church had created a lot of bloodshed in Europe, 100 years wars and 200 years wars. A dark night had descended over Europe with the coming of Christianity. Humanism, rationalism, universalism and all other values which are known as human values had been buried under the dead weight of Christianity. Some people in Europe started questioning the character of Christianity, particularly the stranglehold of the Church over the State. There was a revival of humanism, rationalism and universalism due to Europe's contact with India, China and some other great ancient civilizations. There was a struggle against the Christian Church and over a period of time the State was freed from its stranglehold. It was this struggle which gave birth to the concept of Secularism in Europe. It was a very healthy concept, particularly for those countries which were suffering under the yoke of theocracy, under the inhuman theology of Christianity. This is still a very healthy concept for countries suffering under the yoke of Islam.

But in India today people prescribe Secularism to Hindu society which has never known any religious conflicts, which has never known any religious strife. Recently I was travelling in the Far East and met some Buddhist monks from China. I said to them: "Buddhism came to China from outside. But you had ancient religions of your own. You had Confucianism. You had Taoism. Did Buddhism come in conflict with Confucianism, or Taoism? " They said: "No, never." There was not a single instance of conflict because Confucianism also came from the same deepest source of the Spirit, because Taoism also came from the same source from which Sanatana Dharma springs, from which Jainism springs, from which Vaishnavism springs. All these are different names of the same spiritual message for mankind. I also talked to some people in Japan in order to find out if Buddhism came in conflict with Shintoism which is their ancient religion. They also said, no, the two religions never came into conflict. The two religions are co-existing in mutual harmony till today. I met a taxi driver who was quite an intelligent man. He said: "I am both a Shintoist and a Buddhist." So also in ancient Greece, in ancient Rome, in the whole ancient world, all over Asia and Europe. The world had never known any religious wars before the rise of Christianity.

Religious wars started with the coming of Christianity. They became very, very bloody with the rise of Islam. But Europe had a wave of humanism, rationalism and universalism which broke the stranglehold of Christianity over the State. That is how the concept of Secularism arose. As I have said, it was a very healthy concept in the context of Europe. As a result of it, European society has travelled so far, European science has developed, European technology has developed, and the social welfare system for the people of Europe has improved. All these things have come out of the concept of Secularism.

Hindu society, however, has always been a naturally secular society. Hindu society has never known any theocratic state. You take for instance any Hindu king. You will never find a bigot who favoured this or that sect. Personally he may have belonged to Buddhism or Jainism or Vaishnavism or any other sect. But in his court, in his kingdom, all religions were equally welcome, all religions were equally patronised. In fact, it was the religious people who patronised the king rather than being patronised by him. It was not like the Archbishop of Canterbury who has to wait on the king of England, the king being Defender of the Faith. The Hindu king had to go to rishis, munis and sadhus in order to seek their advice.

It is in such a land, in such a society that the concept of Secularism has been imported from Europe. Not only that. The concept of Secularism has also been turned against Hindu society. Today you know what Secularism means. Whenever the word 'secularism' is uttered, you can sense an anti-Hindu animus. Secularism in India today means denunciation of Hindu society, denunciation of Hindu culture, denunciation of Hindu history. It means denunciation of everything which is Hindu. The word 'Hindu' itself has become a dirty word. In the language of India's Secularism, Muslims are a minority, Christians are a minority. But the Hindus are a "brute" majority. This is the religion of Secularism which is replacing Sanatana Dharma. This is the new vision which has replaced the vision of Sanatana Dharma, the vision of a society and a culture and a history and other things based on Sanatana Dharma.

The excesses of this Secularism, its anti-Hindu animus, have gradually led to a widespread feeling among the Hindus that there is something seriously wrong somewhere. The so-called minorities have become more and more aggressive under the protection of this Secularism. The Christian mission-aries bring billions of dollars into this country from the De-fence and Intelligence and other departments of the govern-ments in Western countries. They spend this mammoth fin-ance for building missions and churches and for making converts. The "light" of Christianity is being spread. So also Islam. Ever since petrodollars have come into play, ever since the Arab nations have become rich, Islam in India which had got a little frightened after the partition in 1947, has reacquired its old self-confidence of the Muslim League days. You have only to read the language press of Islam, particularly the Urdu press, to witness the wave of aggressive self-confidence on which Islamic imperialism is riding at present.

It is due to all these circumstances, due to this seeing through Secularism, due to a renewed aggression from the old imperialist forces which were lying dormant for some time, that Hindu society has experienced some sort of reawakening, some sort of resurgence. We find that Vishwa Hindu Parishad is playing a leading role in consolidating this resurgence, in giving leadership to this resurgence. But I feel that this effort will not get completed, will not acquire a strong core unless the National Vision of the Swadeshi Movement days is recovered, resurrected, reaffirmed and reinterpreted in the new situation. This is what I am trying to do today in my own small measure.

The first thing we have to do to reassert the National Vision, is to proclaim to the whole world, without any fear or hesitation, that this ancient land, this Bharatavarsha is one indivisible whole and that we do not recognise its partition into Afghanistan, Pakistan, Hindustan and Bangladesh. It has often happened in the history of many countries that certain imperialist forces have encroached upon them and have run away with some parts of their lands. We must be very clear in our minds that what are known as Afghanistan, Pakistan and Bangladesh today are parts of the Hindu homeland and that we are going to reclaim them. We should say it fearlessly that the consolidation of Islamic imperialism, a thousand years of Islamic aggression against India, in the shape of Afghanistan, Pakistan and Bangladesh is not going to be tolerated, that sooner or later we shall undo this division of the motherland, and that we shall reclaim our brethren who have been alienated from us by Islamic imperialism.

Some of our people are now known as Muslims, some are known as Christians. All these are our own people. We have nothing against them. But we shall not tolerate imperialism surviving in this country in the form of Islam or in the form of

Christianity. Islamic imperialism has been defeated and dispersed. There is no place for Islam in India today. Christian imperialism has been defeated and dispersed. There is no place for Christianity in India today. We have to say it all in very clear terms.

The second thing which we should say very clearly and fearlessly, is that the history of India is the history of Hindu society, of the Hindu nation, and that we do not recognise any Muslim or British period of this history. We do not recognise any age of Mamluks or Khiljis or Tughlaqs or Lodis or Mughals. We shall instead read our history in terms of our own heroes, in terms of an age of Prithvi Raj Chauhan, an age of Rana Sanga, an age of Krishnadevaraya, an age of Rana Pratap, an age of Shivaji, and so on. We shall not concede that there ever was a Muslim empire in India. We shall instead interpret that period as a long-drawn-out war of national resistance, of national liberation, in which Islamic imperialism was worsted. Similarly, we shall not recognise any British viceroys or governors-general except as imperialist intruders. The imperialist versions of Indian history which are being taught at present in our schools and colleges, have to go.

Take the case of the so-called Muslim empire in India. Within a few years of its prophet's death, Islam had conquered large chunks of Asia and Africa. But it took it 70 long years to put its first step in India, another 500 years to reach Delhi, and a few hundred years more to reach South India, Soon after, Islamic imperialism started retreating before a national struggle for liberation. It started folding up with the rise of Shivaji. So what we had was a long-drawn-out war, a prolonged national struggle against Islamic imperialism. This war, this national struggle should not be described as the Muslim conquest of India or as the Muslim period of Indian history.

The third thing which we have to proclaim in order to reaffirm the National Vision, is that the national culture of India is Hindu culture, the culture of Sanatana Dharma. It is a vast and variegated culture. But at the same time, it is a culture which is natural to mankind. There is nothing artificial about this culture, nothing which has been constructed by the outer mind of man, nothing which has been imposed by force as is the case with the cultures of Christianity and Islam and Communism. Any culture which is not prepared to come to terms with Hindu culture, the culture of Sanatana Dharma, has to go. There is no place for any alien culture to flourish on the soil of India in the name of 'minority rights'.

The fourth thing which we have to proclaim, is that Hindu society is the national society in India. This is a vast society which has permitted endless expressions of human nature, which has sanctioned all types of social traditions. Today we are accused of neglecting our so-called tribals. This is an accusation which is made against us very often. But when you read Hindu history, you find that we never interfered with the life-style of any segment of our society. We wrote 40 Dharmashastras in order to accommodate the customs and traditions and institutions of various regions and communities. Then we wrote 4000 commentaries on the Dharmashastras adapting them to different *jātis*, to different *varṇas*, to different regions. So Hindu society is a vast and complex society. Any community which is not prepared to come to terms with Hindu society has no place in India any more. We shall not permit such alien communities to call themselves minorities and claim special rights and privileges.

Finally, we have to proclaim that the only religion which Hindu society recognises, which has a place in Bharatavarsha, is the natural spirituality of Sanatana Dharma. It is a religion which accommodates all types of human aspirations including atheism, agnosticism, materialism. What it cannot accommodate is force and fraud practised in the name of religion. Any religion which wants to flourish in India has to come to terms with the spirituality of Sanatana Dharma. There is no place in India today for ideologies like Islam and Christianity which harbour imperialist ambitions.

This, then, is the Emerging National Vision. The whole of Bharatavarsha is the Hindu homeland. The history of Bharatavarsha is the history of Hindu society. The national culture of Bharatavarsha is Hindu culture. And the national religion of India is Sanatana Dharma. This is the National Vision which we have to reaffirm.

There are certain implications of this affirmation which we should hold clearly before our minds. Unless we are clear in our minds, unless we are ideologically equipped, unless we acquire knowledge about ourselves as well as about the forces against which we have to fight, the contest will be decided to our disadvantage. Several ideological aggressions have been mounted against Hindu society, against Hindu culture, against Sanatana Dharma in the past as well as in the present. There is the ideological aggression from Christianity. There is the ideological aggression from Islam. There is the ideological aggression from Communism. We have taken a defensive posture against all these aggressions. This will not do.

Today in India, a Hindu has only one *parichaya*, only one name by which he is known. He is known as a communalist. Islamic ideology, Christian ideology, Communist ideology — all of them have made such inroads that a Hindu is being called a communalist in his own homeland. This is the ninth or the tenth wonder of the world. I do not know how many wonders there are in the world at present. But this is surely the greatest wonder of the world. This has happened because Hindus in their ignorance have recognised Islam and Christianity as religions. This recognition has to be withdrawn. This is the first implication of the Emerging National Vision.

Today, by pretending that they are religions, Christianity and Islam are claiming special rights, special privileges, special protection. Take the case of Islam. Its holy books are full of calls for crusades and mass slaughter. Its history has been blood-soaked. Its mosques have always been party offices and arsenals. Yet it pretends that it is a religion. I am not going into the deeper reasons for not regarding Islam and Christianity as religions. The simple fact that both of them divide humanity into mutually exclusive camps of believers and unbelievers, Kafirs and Momins, is sufficient to prove that they are not religions but only political ideologies. They have to be rejected outright. No matter how many libraries have been equipped in defence of these ideologies, no matter how many tons of dogmatics, polemics and apologetics have been marshalled, we have to reject them. We have to proclaim from the housetops that we do not recognise Christianity and Islam as religions.

But we shall not acquire this courage unless we are convinced of the truth of what we have to say. And conviction will not come to us unless we study these so-called religions in depth. I have had an opportunity to study Islam and Christianity under the guidance of Sri Ram Swarup who has a deep knowledge of their so-called scriptures and sacred traditions. There is a lot of theology in these books, there is a lot of ideology. But there is no spirituality in them. Can there be a religion without spirituality? Religion has something to do with man's spiritual quest, has something to do with man's soul, with man's deeper drives, with man's larger and loftier aspirations. But we find nothing of this sort in the books of Christianity and Islam. What we find there is political ideologies of aggression, what we find there is imperialist ambitions of conquering and converting other people by force.

The second implication of the Emerging National Vision is that Muslims and Christians who have been forced into the fold of alien ideologies, into the fold of imperialist ideologies masquerading as religions, have to be brought back to their ancestral fold. These are our own people. When we reject Islam, we do not reject Muslims. When we reject Christianity, we do not reject Christians. They are our own flesh and blood. They have to be rescued from the prison-houses of Islam and Christianity, from the dark dungeons of deadening fanaticism.

These are the implications which we should understand very clearly. Hindu society has to be ideologically equipped. It has to know its own history, its own scriptures, its own culture in depth and width, its own identity as a nation. At the same time, it has to know from the horse's mouth, from the original sources, the character of Islam and Christianity, the character of Communism, and the character of modern materialism which is now coming to us as American Consumerism. Unless we have this knowledge, the battle will not be really joined.

The old enemies will use the old weapons over and over again so long as Hindu society remains on the defensive. They will go on calling us communalists, etc. Hindu society has been on the defensive since 1920 when the Congress took up the cause of Khilafat. Since then Islam and other alien forces have been on the offensive. Islam has been saying that it stands for monotheism while Hinduism stands for polytheism, that it stands for a casteless society while Hinduism stands for caste hierarchy, and so on. Now if we do not know the character of Hindu society, the character of Varnashrama Dharma and how this social system has been our great saviour throughout our history, we are taken in.

Very few people know that the Muslims in India have always divided their own society into three separate sections, apart from the fact that there are as many, if not more, castes among the Muslims as among the Hindus. The descendents of foreign invaders like the Arabs, the Turks and the Persians are known among the Muslims as *ashrāf* which is the plural of *sharīf*, which means the noble ones, the exalted ones. The converts from the higher Hindu castes like the Brahmins and Rajputs are known as *ajlāf*. And the converts from the lower Hindu castes are known as *arzāl* which is the plural of *razīl*, which means the ignoble, the mean. This common language of casteism among the Muslims, we do not know. Therefore, when they talk of Hindu society as caste-ridden and their own society as casteless, we are taken in.

Again, take for instance this Islamic talk about monotheism. This is a monstrous idea. It is not a spiritual idea at all. It puts God above the cosmos and makes all manifestation bereft of divinity. This is a theological idea. This is an intellectual concept. But we have been trying to prove all these days that we are also monotheists. We have to know the spirituality of Sanatana Dharma as also the ideology of Islam in order to see through monotheism and to reject it as an intellectual bluff.

An ideological battle has to be waged in order to avoid the other battle, the physical battle. Societies which fail to fight an ideological battle, which refuse to repel ideological aggression, invite physical aggression sooner or later. If ideological aggression is not stopped, a society gets taken for granted and physical aggression follows. This is the law of Nature. We did not fight against the ideological aggression of the Muslim League which was later on joined by the Communist Party of India (CPI). It was the CPI which collected facts and figures and gave respectability to the ideological aggression from Islam. I know it personally because I was myself a Communist at that time. And we know what happened. Physical aggression followed. The country was partitioned. Millions were rendered homeless, millions were killed.

So, if we want to save our society from physical aggression, from physical clashes, from street riots, from bloodshed, we should take up this ideological battle immediately. But we have to be equipped in order to fight this battle. We have to know our own Hindu society, our own Hindu culture, our own Hindu history, our own Sanatana Dharma. We have also to know Islam and Christianity and Communism from their own sources, from the horse's mouth. We should not have any private versions of these alien ideologies. We should know them as they are in themselves, as expounded by their own spokesmen.

We Hindus have a very bad habit, a suicidal habit, of finding in our own traditions, in our own scriptures, whatever the alien ideologies claim for themselves. We try to find Christianity in our scriptures, we try to find Islam in our scriptures, we try to find Communism in our scriptures. This is a very bad habit. We must know the enemy as he is. Otherwise the ideological battle is not really joined.

Today in India, Christianity is ideologically equipped. Over that last so many years, Christian missionaries have been studying Hindu religion, Hindu society and Hindu culture and tearing them to bits. They know when and where to attack, when and where to retreat. They know all the strategic points. They know all the tactics. Islam has not been studying our religion or society or culture. But it knows that when it says that it stands for monotheism, that it stands for equality, that it stands for human brotherhood, the Hindu tends to run away. Whenever Islam calls the Hindu a communalist, the Hindu runs away. So far as its own ideology is concerned, Islam has a lot of centres where Islam is taught in depth and detail. A lot of finance is also available for these centres. New Islamic universities are coming up. You may have read in the newspapers that a 15 crore scheme has been made for an Islamic Cultural Centre in New Delhi. Hidayatullah has spoken about it. The money will come from the Islamic Cooperative Bank floated by the Arabs. The Government of India will also make a contribution.

But there is not a single Hindu centre worth the name in India. We have lots of ashramas and mathas and some publishing houses. We have many swamis and lots of talk about Hindu religion and Hindu culture. But there is no Hindu centre which develops Hindu scholarship , which studies the whole range of Hindu heritage, which tries to know and to make known Islam and Christianity and Communism inside out. There is no Hindu centre which can provide comparative studies and a clarity of vision and which can equip us for an ideological battle. The National Vision which is emerging has not only to be reaffirmed, it has also to be ideologically equipped.

As I come to the end of my talk today, I should like to add one more point. We should not see this ideological battle as taking place in India alone. That will narrow down our perspective. The ideological battle which is taking place in India is part of a worldwide battle. We are not alone. We also have our allies abroad. Our allies are not foreign governments and foreign financial institutions. Our greatest ally is the indomitable and immortal human spirit, the deeper culture of the human soul. The wave of humanism, rationalism and universalism which has been sweeping over the Western world is our strongest ally. Christianity, for instance, is almost dead in the West today. They give money to the Christian missions under the mistaken impression that the missionaries are doing social service in India. But if we make it known to the West, to the people over there, that the Christian missionaries are using this money for subverting Hindu society and Hindu culture, we shall find many allies.

Islam is a hard nut to crack because Islam is still living in a world of die-hard dogmatism. Islamic lands are under a deep spell of darkness. It is very difficult to penetrate these lands physically. We can go into the homelands of Christianity. We can speak to them, we can appeal to them, we can discuss with them. Their minds have opened up. But the mind of Islam is a closed mind. It is not easy to open it up.

I have discussed this problem of Islam with Sri Ram Swarup. He says that ideas can penetrate every wall, travel everywhere. Maybe we are unable to go physically into Islamic lands with our message of humanism, rationalism and universalism. But we can give a call to them to throw away their closed creed and feel free. We can invite them into the open sunshine of natural spirituality which is Sanatana Dharma. The Islamic lands are in the throes of a deep crisis. Most of their students who go to Western universities, who come to Indian universities, do not want to go back to their Islamic countries, Iran and Iraq and so on. They find the atmosphere at home suffocating. They are our allies.

So we should not see this ideological battle which is raging in India today in isolation. It is a worldwide battle. Christianity has its allies abroad. Islam has its allies abroad. So has Communism. But we also have our allies abroad. Our allies may not have money as their allies have. Our allies may not have physical power, military power, as their allies have. But

we must remember that our ally is the human spirit everywhere. We must appeal to this human spirit, seek succour from
this human spirit, as we go into an ideological battle. We are
bound to win.

I thank you all for giving me a patient hearing, for sparing
so much of your time.

Appendix – 2

Plea for Study of Islamic Polity in India's Universities

To
The Chairman
University Grants Commission,
Bahadur Shah Zafar Marg,
New Delhi-110002

Sub: Inclusion of the study of Islamic Concept
of State in the syllabus of Political Science prescribed
for the students of B.A. and M.A. classes.

Sir,

I am writing this letter for your consideration after carefully studying the contents of the subject of Political Science which is being taught to our students in various universities in the country.

1. You must be aware, as many others are, that the most truculent problem that our country has been facing for more than a hundred years is the problem of Muslims, their aspirations, their proneness to violence, their dislike of dissent and debate, and their undying belief that gun and sword is the ultimate arbiter. No sooner, one demand of the Muslims in India is conceded that another is raised. This situation cannot be better illustrated than by the classic observation of Mr. H.S. Suhrawardy, one

time Prime Minister of United Bengal just before the notorious Direct Action of August 16, 1946 in Calcutta, that "Pakistan is not our last demand but our latest demand". More than 5000 Hindus and Muslims were killed as a result of this Direct Action launched by the Muslim League. Has the creation of Pakistan solved the Muslim/communal problem? The answer is an emphatic No. But why? The one and only reason is that our academia, for unknown reasons, has over the years, totally neglected the study of the Islamic Concept of State or Khilafat as if such a concept does not exist either in the world of political thought or Islamic theology. Nations which have a proper understanding of this concept have dealt with Muslim problems much more effectively and much better than us.

2. This deficiency in the teaching of Political Science in our universities has been of monumental proportions. In fact, while no attention has been paid to this aspect, a certain class of intellectuals react to any such suggestion with utmost disdain and contempt. No wonder, that several generations of all communities and Hindus in particular, have paid a terribly heavy price in terms of unmitigated violence, bloodshed and "ethnic cleansing" of Himalayan dimensions. If the future generations have to be protected against such violence then the study of Islamic Theory of State or Khilafat must be included in the relevant syllabi. Future generations will be enlightened about the source and wellsprings of violence and why the Muslim problem has remained so vicious in spite of herculean efforts made by Mahatma Gandhi who failed to win over the Muslims resulting in disastrous consequences for the Indian nation including his dastardly assassination.

3. The proposed subjects of study would include the following:
   i. Islamic Concept of State/Khilafat and its history.

    ii. The role of violence in an Islamic state.

   iii. The duties of a ruler in an Islamic state.

   iv. Human Rights in an Islamic state.

    v. Position of minorities in an Islamic state.

   vi. Dissidence and debate in an Islamic state.

  vii. The role of Fatwas in an Islamic state.

 viii. The concepts of Jihad, Jiziyah, Ghanimah (Plunder), Dar-ul-Harb and Dar-ul-Islam.

   ix. The Quranic concept of war.

    x. Banking and Usury.

   xi. Plurality vs Hijrat.

4. All this and more is an integral part of the overarching Islamic political thought. Its study has now become imperative in national interest and should no more be neglected. Such calamities as partition of India and the Kashmir problem (which is now 50 years old) could have been avoided by proper study and evaluation of Islamic political thought.

5. The Islamic State/Khilafat has four clear cut periods which are as follows:

    i. First Khilafat – Period of pure theocracy 632 to 661 A.D.

   ii. Second Khilafat – 661 to 1258 A.D. The Khilafat took the shape of hereditary temporal dominion.

  iii. Third Khilafat – 1258 to 1517 A.D. The Khilafat had no sovereign rights, and temporal authority was wielded by Mamluk Sultans of Egypt and Muslim Princes.

  iv. Fourth and last Khilafat (Ottomon) 1517 to 1921 A.D. Abolished by Mustafa Kamal.

There is no reason why the study of Khilafat alongwith Platonic, Christian and Marxist concepts of state must not be made compulsory.

Thus, in view of the foregoing, you are requested to kindly advise or direct the universities all over the country to take immediate steps in this regard. Those willing to do so will soon realise how grossly deficient their knowledge of the subject had been.

In the end, it may also be mentioned that there is no dearth of excellent books on the subject by both Muslim and non-Muslim authors.

Kindly acknowledge receipt.

Copy to:-
1. Vice-Chancellors of all universities in India.
2. Heads of Departments of Political Science in all Universities in India

Chandigarh   Yours truly,
5 September 1998   Baljit Rai IPS (Retd.)

Appendix – 3

Scriptural Sanctions for the Behaviour Pattern of the Followers of Biblical or Prophetic Monotheism

Sources

1. *Good News Bible: Today's English Version*, Bible Society of India, Bangalore, n.d.
2. *The meaning of the Glorious Quran*, Text, Translation and Commentary by Abdullah Yusuf Ali, Dār al-Kitāb al-Misri, Cairo, Third Edition, 2 volumes, 1938.
3. *Sīrat Rasūl Allāh* of Ibn Ishāq, translated into English as *The Life of Muhammad* by A. Gillaume (1955), OUP, Karachi, Eighth Impression, 1987.
4. *The Rauzat-us-Safa* or, *Garden of Purity* of Muhammad Khavendshāh bin Mahmūd, translated into English by E. Rehatsek (1893), Delhi reprint, Part II, Volume Second, 1982.
5. *The Hedaya*, Commentary on Islamic Law, translated by Charles Hamilton (London, 1791), New Delhi reprint, Volume II, 1985.
6. Hughes, Thomas Patrick, *Dictionary of Islam* (1885), New Delhi reprint, 1976.
7. *Sahih Muslim* of Imam Muslim, cited in *Dictionary of Islam*.
8. *Miskāt* of Imam al-Umri, cited in *Dictionary of Islam*.

9. *Zhakhiratu'l-Muluk* of Saiyid 'Ali Hamadani, cited in *A History of Sufism in India* by Saiyid Athar Abbas Rizvi, Volume I, New Delhi, 1978.

10. *Tabqāt-i-Ibn Sa'd,* translated into Urdu by Allāma 'Abdullāh al-Ahmadī, 2 Parts, Karachi, 1982

Misleading (Mischievous?) Translations

The Being who communicates with Moses in the Bible identifies himself as YHWH. Exodus 3.13-15 reads: "But Moses replied, 'When I go to the Israelites and say to them, the God of your ancestors sent me to you, they will ask me, What is his name? So what can I tell them?' God said, 'I am who I am. This is what you must say to them: The one who is called I AM has sent me to you.' Tell the Israelites that I, the LORD, the God of their ancestors, the God of Abraham, Issac, and Jacob, have sent you to them. This is my name for ever; this is what all future generations are to call me" (*Good News Bible, The old Testament* p. 61). The translators explain in a footnote: "*'I am' sounds like the Hebrew name Yahweh traditionally transliterated as Jehovah. This name is represented in this translation by 'the LORD' in capital letters, following a usage which is widespread in English versions*" (Ibid., n.*e*. Emphasis in original). But as they themselves point out in the Preface, the Hebrew language has a distinct word meaning 'Lord' — *Adonai* (Ibid., p. viii). Another modern translation says the same thing: "The word LORD when spelled with capital letters, stands for the divine name YHWH, which is here connected with the verb *hayah*, to be" (*The Holy Bible: Revised Standard Version*, New York, n.d., p. 58). The translators of this version, however, admit quite frankly: "The use of any proper name for the *one and only God*, as though there were other gods from whom he had to be distinguished, was discontinued in Judaism before the Christian era and is entirely inappropriate for the universal faith of the Christian Church" (Ibid., p. vii. Emphasis added). *The Revised Standard Version* also points out that the Hebrew word "Elohim" has been rendered as "God" in all English translations (Ibid., p.vi).

We wonder, in the absence of an explanation in the foregoing apology, as to why the use of the proper name, YHWH, was "discontinued in Judaism". But whatever may be the explanation, the fact remains that YHWH of the Bible is a Being who has his Chosen People as well as a hit list of his enemies. To pass off such a questionable character as *LORD* is absolutely dishonest. So also the attempt to pass off "Elohim" as "God". The words "Lord" as well as "God" are Germanic in origin and were used, as we shall explain, in a polytheistic and pantheistic context by the Pagan Germans before they were forced into the fold of Christianity. In fact, the word "God" is from Indo-European, and is cognate with the Sanskrit word "*Huta*", meaning "he to whom oblations are offered".

Similar is the case with the word "Allah" which has been uniformly translated as "God" in the English version of the Quran we have used. Most English translations of the Quran have been doing the same for years on end. The first half of the *Kalimah* itself has been translated into English to read "There is no god but God", which is mischievous to say the least. The correct translation should be "There is no god but Allah". It is true that Allah is a composite Arabic word which means The (*Al*) God (*Lāh*). In the pre-Islamic Arabic language, Allāh was the Supreme God of the Pagan Arab pantheon which had many other Gods and Goddesses. But the word "Allah" started having an altogether different meaning when Muhammad, the Last Prophet according to the Quran, hijacked it from the ancient Arab language and used it as a synonym for YHWH of the Bible. Allah of the Quran claims again and again that he is the same Being who had made revelations to the Jewish prophets, who had spoken at length to Moses when he led the Jews out of Egypt and towards "the Promised Land" in Palestine, and who had sent Jesus as the prophet of the Christians. We agree with the

Government of Malaysia which has enacted a law that the word "Allah" should not be translated into any other word, and should remain as such in all translations of Islamic scriptures.

What is more important, the conceptual context in which the words "Lord" and "God" and "Allah" were used by the pre-Christian German Pagans and the pre-Islamic Arab Pagans, was radically different from that imposed on these words by the Bible and the Quran. We have to make the following observations on the conceptional context:

    i. In the Pagan context, these words stood for a Supreme God who transcended the Cosmos at the same time that he was immanent in it. In the Biblical and the Quranic context, on the other hand, these words have been used for a Being who is extra-Cosmic and for whom both transcendence as well as immanence are blasphemous notions.

    ii. In the Pagan context, these words signified the Great God who presided over a pantheon of numerous Gods and Goddesses, who shared his divinity with members of his pantheon, and who could be worshipped through any God or Goddess. Moreover, he as well as members of his pantheon, could be worshipped in many forms including those of birds, animals, trees, plants, rocks — male or female, animate or inanimate, carved or uncarved. In the Biblical and Quranic context, on the other hand, these words denote a Being who stands alone without any pantheon, who shares his attributes only with himself, and who cannot be worshipped in any form whatsoever. Moreover, the Being of the Bible and the Quran is a male chauvinist, particularly hostile to female deities who were worshipped widely in areas where these two scriptures took shape and worked havoc.

    iii. In the Pagan context, these words denoted a Gracious God who was directly accessible to whosoever sought for him sincerely through any spiritual discipline suited to the seeker's stage of moral and spiritual development. In the Biblical and the Quranic context, on the other hand, these words stand for a Being who is accessible only to some privileged persons, known as prophets and chosen by him arbitrarily without any reference to the moral and spiritual qualifications of the persons thus honoured. All other human beings have to learn about him and his commandments through the mouth of the prophets.

iv. In the Pagan context, these words stood for a Universal God who was equally benevolent to all creation, human as well as non-human, who showered his favours on whosoever sought his help with love, devotion and good works, and who did not call for faith in any intermediary. In the Biblical and the Quranic context, on the other hand, the words mean a partisan Being who has his Chosen People as well as his Chosen Enemies, and who commands the former to wage a permanent war for destroying the latter root and branch. He does not care for the moral and spiritual merits of the people in the two camps; his choice depends only on one criterion — acceptance or repudiation of his latest prophet.

We have, therefore, replaced the words "Lord" and "God" with the words "Jehovah" and "Elohim" in our citations from the English translation of the Bible, and with the words "Rabb" and "Allah" in our citations from the English translation of the Quran.

Next, there are Arabic words in the verses we have cited from the Quran, which have been mistranslated to suit the convenience of modern Islamic Apologetics. The following may be noted as examples:

i. *Qatl*: The Arabic word *"qatl"* means "murder"

(*Dictionary*, pp. 420-21, 479). Even in the Urdu
language which has borrowed the word from Arabic,
the word stands simply for killing, slaying murder,
etc. But in the verses we have cited from the English
translation, it has been rendered as "fight" in 2.190,
193, 216, 244; 3.146; 4.74, 76, 84; 8.39, 65; 9.12,
29, 36, 123. In 2.191, on the other hand, it has been
rendered as "slay". The cat comes out of the bag in
9.111 where at one point the word has been
rendered as "fight" but at another point as "slay".
Also in 3.169 and 47.4.

ii. *Kāfir*: The Arabic word "*kāfir*" literally means
"the coverer". "The word is generally used by
Muhammadans to define one who is an unbeliever
in the ministry of Muhammad and his Qur'ān, and
in this sense it has been used by Muhammad
himself " (*Dictionary*, p. 259). In the verses we
have cited from the English translation, however,
this word has been rendered variously as "those
who reject faith" (2.257, 9.3, 47.8), "those who
suppress faith" (2.191), "those who resist faith"
(3.147, 5.39), "those who reject our Signs" (4.56),
"those who blaspheme" (5.75), "those who resist
God" (8.14), "unfaith" (9.12), and "those who reject
God" (4.78, 9.2, 47.34). The translator has thus
been arbitrary as well as inconsistent. The word
"faith" in the translation serves for the Arabic word
"*īmān*", which means "confession of the lips to the
truth of the Muslim religion" (Ibid., p. 204). The
word "God" used by the translator is a mistrans-
lation of the word "Allah", as we have already
pointed out.

iii. *Tāghūt*: The Dictionary of Islam (p. 625) defines
Tāghūt as "An idol mentioned in the Qur'ān (2.257,
2.59, 4.54)" and says further that according to
Jalaluddin "*Tāghūt* was an idol of the Quraish". But

in the translation cited by us it has been rendered as "Evil" with capital E (2.257, 4.76, 16.36, 39.17). This is mischievous. The idol under reference might have been denounced by Muhammad, but for the Arab Pagans it represented a divinity. The translator should have retained the proper name and not forced it to mean the opposite of what it meant to those who had installed it.

There are many other tricks played by this translator in his translation as a whole, particularly when he uses brackets for interpolating words which are not there in the Arabic text. In short, the whole of this translation is an exercise in Apologetics, as is quite clear if one refers to the copious footnotes on every page.

ICONOCLASM

The Bible

1. Then Moses said to Jehovah," The People cannot come up, because you commanded us to consider the mountain sacred and to mark a boundary round it"... Jehovah spoke and these were his words: "I am Jehovah your Elohim who brought you out of Egypt, where you were slaves. Worship no god but me. Do not make for yourselves images of anything in heaven or on earth or in the water under the earth. Do not bow down to any idol or worship it, because I am Jehovah your Elohim and I tolerate no rivals. I bring punishment on those who hate me and on their descendants down to the third and fourth generation. But I show my love to thousands of generations of those who love me and obey my laws." (Exodus, 19:23; 20.1-6)

2. Jehovah commanded Moses to say to the Israelites: "... You have seen how I, Jehovah, have spoken to you from heaven. Do not make for yourselves gods of silver or gold to be worshipped in addition to me... My angel will go ahead of you and take you into the land of the Amorites, the Hittites, the

Perizzites, the Canaanites, the Hivites, the Jebusites, and I will destroy them. Do not bow down to their gods or worship them and do not adopt their religious practices. Destroy their gods and break down their sacred stone pillars." (Exodus, 20:22-23; 23:23-24)

3. When Moses came close enough to the camp to see the bull-calf and to see the people dancing, he was furious... He took the bull-calf which they had made, melted it, ground it into fine powder, and mixed it with water. Then he made the people of Israel drink it. (Exodus, 32:19, 20)

4. Then Moses said to the people... "When Jehovah spoke to you from the fire on Mount Sinai, you did not see any form. For your own good, then make certain that you do not sin by making for yourselves an idol in any form at all — whether man or woman, animal or bird, reptile or fish. Do not be tempted to worship and serve what you see in the sky — the sun, the moon and the stars. Jehovah your Elohim has given these to all other peoples for them to worship. But you are the people he rescued from Egypt, that blazing furnace... Be certain that you do not forget the covenant that Jehovah your Elohim made with you.... Be certain that you do. Obey his command not to make yourselves any kind of idol because Jehovah your Elohim is like a flaming fire; he tolerates no rivals. (Deuteronomy, 4:1, 15-20, 23, 24)

5. "Honour Jehovah your Elohim, worship only him and make your promises in his name alone. Do not worship other gods, any of the gods of the peoples around you. If you do worship other gods, Jehovah's anger will come against you like fire and will destroy you completely, because Jehovah your Elohim, who is present with you, tolerates no rivals. (Deuteronomy, 6:13-15)

6. "Jehovah your Elohim will bring you into the land which you are going to occupy, and he will drive many nations out of it. As you advance, he will drive out seven nations larger and more powerful than you... When Jehovah your Elohim places these people in your power and you defeat them, you must put

them all to death. Do not make any alliance with them or show them any mercy. Do not marry any of them, and do not let your children marry any of them, because then they would lead your children away from Jehovah to worship other gods. If that happens, Jehovah will be angry with you and destroy you at once. So then, tear down their altars, break their sacred stone pillars in pieces, cut down the symbols of their goddess Asherah, and burn their idols. Do this because you belong to Jehovah your Elohim. From all the peoples on earth he chose you to be his own special people... He will put their kings in your power. You will kill them, and they will be forgotten. No one will be able to stop you; you will destroy everyone. Burn their idols. Do not desire the silver or gold that is on them, and do not take it for yourselves. If you do, that will he be fatal, because Jehovah hates idolatry. Do not bring any of these idols into your homes, or the same curse will be on you that is on them. You must hate and despise those idols, because they are under Jehovah's curse. (Deuteronomy, 7: 1-6, 24-26)

7. Moses called together all the people of Israel and said to them, "People of Israel, listen to all the laws that I am giving you today... Here are the laws that you are to obey as long as you live in the land that Jehovah, the Elohim of your ancestors, is giving you. Listen to them! In the land that you are taking, destroy all the places where the people worship their gods on high mountains, on hills and under green trees. Tear down their altars and smash their sacred stone pillars to pieces. Burn their symbols of the goddess Asherah and chop down their idols, so that they will never again be worshipped at those places ... Even your brother or your son or your daughter or the wife you love or your closest friend may secretly encourage you to worship other gods, gods that you and your ancestors have never worshipped . One of them may encourage you to worship the gods of those who live near you or the gods of those who live far away. But do not let him persuade you; do not even listen to him. Show him no mercy or pity, and do not protect him. Kill him! Be the first to stone

him, and then let everyone else stone him too. Stone him to
death! He tried to lead you away from Jehovah your Elohim,
who rescued you from Egypt, where you were slaves. Then all
the people of Israel will hear what happened; they will be
afraid, and no one will ever again do such an evil thing.
(Deuteronomy, 5:1; 12:1-3; 13:6-11)

8. "When you are living in the towns that Jehovah your
Elohim gives you, you may hear that some worthless men of
your nation have misled the people of their town to worship
gods that you have never worshipped before. If you hear
such a rumour, investigate it thoroughly; and if it is true that
this evil thing did happen, then kill all the people in that town
completely. Bring together all the possessions of the people
who live there and pile them up in the town square. Then
burn the town and everything in it as an offering to Jehovah
your Elohim. It must be left in ruins for ever and never again
rebuilt . (Deuteronomy, 13:12-16)

9. "But when you capture cities in the land that Jehovah
your Elohim is giving you, kill everyone. Completely destroy
all the people: the Hittites, the Amorites, the Canaanites, the
Perizzites, the Hivites, and the Jebusites, as Jehovah ordered
you to do. Kill them, so that they will not make you sin
against Jehovah by teaching you to do all the disgusting
things that they do in the worship of their gods." (Deuteronomy, 20:16-18)

10. Then Moses said to the people of Israel, "... The
Levites will speak these words in a loud voice: Elohim's
curse on anyone who makes an idol of stone, wood, or metal
and secretly worships it. Jehovah hates idolatry." (Deuteronomy,
27:11, 15)

11. Stephen answered "... It was then that they made an
idol in the shape of a bull, offered sacrifice to it, and had a
feast in honour of what they themselves had made. So
Elohim turned away from them." (Acts, 7:41-42)

12. My children, keep yourselves safe from false gods!
(1 John, 5:21)

13. Do not try to work together as equals with the unbelievers, for it cannot be done. How can right and wrong be partners? How can light and darkness live together? How can Christ and Devil agree? What does a believer have in common with an unbeliever? How can Elohim's temple come to terms with pagan idols? For we are the temple of the living Elohim! (2 Corinthians, 6:16)

14. All those people speak about... how you [Thessalonians] turned away from idols to Elohim, to serve the true and living Elohim... (1 Thessalonians,1:9)

The Quran

15. No partner has He [Allah]: This am I commanded, and I am the first of those who bow to His will. (Quran, 6:163)

16. And remember We took a covenant from the children of Israel (to this effect): worship none [no other god] but Allah. (Quran, 2:83)

17. For we assuredly sent amongst every people an apostle (with the commandment), "Serve Allah, and eschew Tāghūt..." So travel through the earth, and see what was the end of those who denied the Truth. Shun the abomination of idols. (Quran, 16:36; 22:30)

18. Say: "We [Muslims] worship none but Allah; we associate no partners with Him. Soon shall we cast terror into the hearts of the Unbelievers for that they joined companions with Allah... Their abode will be the Fire." (Quran, 3:64, 151)

19. We took the Children of Israel (with safety) across the sea. They came upon a people devoted entirely to some idols they had. They said: "O Moses ! fashion for us a god like unto the gods they have." He said: "Surely you are a people without knowledge. As to these folk, — the cult they are in is (but) a fragment of a ruin, and vain is the (worship) which they practise." He said: "Shall I seek for you a god other than Allah, when it is Allah who has endowed you with gifts above the nations ?" ... The people of Moses made in his absence, out of their ornaments, the image of a calf (for worship)... They took

it for worship and they did wrong... When Moses came back to his people, angry and grieved, he said: "Evil it is that you have done in my place in my absence... Those who took the calf (for worship) will indeed be overwhelmed with wrath from their Rabb and with shame in this life. Thus we do recompense those who invent (falsehoods)... He prayed: "O my Rabb!... Would you destroy us for the deeds of the foolish ones among us... So forgive us and give us your mercy; for you are the best of those who forgive... He said: "With My Punishment I visit whom I will." (Quran, 7:138-140, 148, 150, 152, 155, 156)*

20. Lo! Abraham said to his father Āzar: "Take you idols for gods? For I see you and your people in manifest error." (Quran, 6:74)

21. And rehearse to them (something of) Abraham's story. Behold! he said to his father and his people: " What worship you?" They said: "We worship idols, and we remain constantly in attendance on them." He said: "Do they listen to you when you call or do you good or harm?" They said: "Nay, but we found our fathers doing thus." He said: "Do you then see whom you have been worshipping, you and your fathers before you? For they are enemies to me." (Quran, 26:70-77)

22. And he (Abraham) said: "For you, you have taken (for worship) idols besides Allah out of mutual love and regard between yourselves in this life; but on the Day of Judgement you shall disown each other and curse each other: and your abode will be the Fire, and you shall have none to help." (Quran, 29:25)

23. We bestowed aforetime on Abraham his rectitude of conduct. Behold! he said to his father and his people, "What are these images, to which you are devoted ?" They said, "We found our fathers worshipping them." He said, "Indeed you have been in manifest Error — you and your fathers. ... And by Allah, I have a plan for your idols, after you go away and turn your backs." So he broke them to pieces, (all) but the

---

*This story of the Golden Calf is repeated in 20:82-99.

biggest of them... (Abraham) said, "Do you then worship, besides Allah, things that can neither be of any good to you nor do you harm? Fie upon you, and upon the things that you worship besides Allah ! Have you no sense?" They said, "Burn him and protect your gods." ... We said, "O Fire! Be you cool, and (a means of) safety for Abraham!" Then they sought a stratagem against him: but We made them the ones that lost most. But we delivered him... (Quran, 21:51-54, 57-58, 66-71)

24. Noah said: "O my Rabb! They have disobeyed me... And they have said (to each other), 'abandon not your gods.'... They have already misled many; and grant you no increase to the wrong-doers but in straying (from their mark)." Because of their sins they were drowned (in the flood), and were made to enter the Fire (of Punishment): and they found — in lieu of Allah — none to help them. And Noah said: "O my Rabb! Leave not of the Unbelievers a single one on earth! For if You do leave (any of) them, they will but mislead Your devotees, and they will breed none but wicked ungrateful ones." (Quran, 71:21, 23-27)

25. Behold, Luqman said to his son by way of instruction: "O my son! join not in worship (others) with Allah: for false worship is indeed the highest wrong-doing." (Quran, 31:13)

26. He is the Living (One): there is no god but He ... Say: "I have been forbidden to invoke those whom you invoke besides Allah..." Those who reject the Book and the (revelations) with which We sent Our apostles: but soon shall they know, when the yokes (shall be) round their necks, and the chains, they shall be dragged along in the boiling fetid fluid; then in the Fire shall they be burned; then shall it be said to them: "Where are the (deities) to which you gave part worship — in derogation of Allah... Enter you the gates of Hell, to dwell therein: and evil is (this) abode of the arrogant". (Quran, 40:65, 66, 70-74, 76)

27. Allah has said: "Take not (for worship) two gods: for He is just One Allah: then fear Me (and Me alone)." (Quran, 16:51)

28. Serve Allah, and join not any partners with Him... To set up partners with Allah is to devise a sin most heinous indeed. Allah forgives not (the sin of) joining other gods with Him; but He forgives, to whom He pleases other sins than this: one who joins other gods with Allah, has strayed far, far away (from the Right)... (Quran, 4:36, 48, 116)

29. ... Of those who reject faith the patrons are the Tāghūt: from light they will lead them forth into the depths of darkness. They will be the companions of the Fire, to dwell therein (for ever). (Quran, 2:257)

30. ...invoke not, with Allah, any other god... and any that does this (not only) meets punishment (but) the penalty on the Day of Judgement will be doubled to him, and he will dwell therein in ignominy. (Quran, 25:68-69)

31. These are among the (precepts of) wisdom, which your Rabb has revealed to you. Take not, with Allah, another object of worship, lest you should be thrown into Hell, blameworthy and rejected. (Quran, 17:39)

32. Those who eschew Tāghūt and fall not into its worship, and turn to Allah (in repentance), for them is Good News: So announce the Good News to My servants... The Unbelievers will be led to Hell in crowd... (To them) will be said: "Enter you the gates of Hell, to dwell therein: and evil is (this) abode of the arrogant!" (Quran, 39:17, 71-72)

33. And the places of worship are for Allah alone. So invoke not any one along with Allah... Say: "I do no more than invoke my Rabb, and I join not with Him any (false god)... For any that disobey Allah and His Apostle, — for them is Hell: they shall dwell therein for ever." (Quran, 72:18, 20, 23)

Sunnah of the Prophet of Islam:

34. The apostle entered Mecca on the day of the conquest and it contained 360 idols which Iblīs had strengthened with lead. The apostle was standing by them with a stick in his hand, saying, 'The truth has come and falsehood has passed

away; verily falsehood is sure to pass away' (*Sūra* 17.82). Then he pointed at them with his stick and they collapsed on their backs one after the other.

When the apostle prayed the noon prayer on the day of the conquest he ordered that all the idols which were round the Ka'ba should be collected and burned with fire and broken up. Faḍāla b. al-Mulawwiḥ al-Layathi said commemorating the day of the conquest:

> Had you seen Muhammad and his troops
> The day the idols were smashed when he entered,
> You would have seen Allah's light become manifest
> And darkness covering the face of idolatry. (Ibn Isḥāq,

p. 552)

35. Then the apostle sent Khālid to al-'Uzzā which was in Nakhla. "It was a temple which this tribe of Quraysh and Kināna and al-Muḍar used to venerate. Its guardians and warders were B. Shaybān of B. Sulaym, allies of B. Hāshim... When Khālid arrived he destroyed her and returned to the apostle. (Ibid., p. 565)

36. The proclaimer authorised by the Prophet of Allah went throughout calling upon all those who believe in Allah and the Last Day to leave no idol unbroken in their homes. (*Tabqāt-i-Ibn Sa'd*, Volume I, p. 478)

37. The Prophet sent expeditions to those idols which were in the neighbourhood and had them destroyed; these included al-'Uzza, Manāt, Suwā, Buāna and Dhu'l-Kaffayn (Ibid.)

38. It is related in some biographies that while the siege of Tāyf was being carried on, his holy and prophetic lordship appointed A'li Murtadza with a number of glorious companions to make excursions into the country, and to destroy every idol they could find... Thereon A'li, the Commander of the Faithful... destroyed all the idols of the Bani Hoāzān and Bani Thaqyf which were in that region. The apostle was waiting for his return near the gate of the fort of Tāyf, and as soon as the prince of saints had terminated his business, he joined the august camp, was received by the seal of prophets

with the exclamation of the *Takbyr...* (*The Rauzat-us-Safa*, pp. 630-631).

39. Among the things they [the envoys of the Arab tribe of Thaqīf] asked the apostle was that they should be allowed to retain their idol Al-Lāt undestroyed for three years. The apostle refused, and they continued to ask him for a year or two, and he refused; finally they asked for a month after their return home; but he refused to agree to any set time. All that they wanted as they were trying to show was to be safe from their fanatics and women and children by leaving her, and they did not want to frighten their people by destroying her [the idol of the goddess Al-Lāt] until they had accepted Islam. The apostle refused this... When they had accomplished their task [of embracing Islam] and had set out to return to their country the apostle sent with them Abū Sufyān and al-Mughīra to destroy the idol... When al-Mughīra entered he went up to the idol and struck it with a pick-axe... When al-Mughīra had destroyed her [the idol] and taken what was on her and her jewels he sent for Abū Sufyān when her jewellery and gold and beads had been collected. (Ibn Ishāq, pp. 615-617)

40. A deputation of nineteen men from Banū Hanīfa came to the Prophet of Allah... They were treated well... These people presented themselves to the Prophet in the mosque... and received instruction in the Quran... When they intended to return, the Prophet ordered that each one of them be given five ounces of silver as a gift... When they got ready to return the Prophet gave them a vessel which contained water left over from his ablutions, and he said, "When you return to your country, destroy the church, wash the site with this water, and build a mosque on it." These people did accordingly. Talq bin 'Ali became the *muazzin*. He gave the *azān*. The priest incharge heard it, and said that it was an invitation to truth, and ran away. His days were over. (*Tabqāt-i-Ibn Sa'd*, Volume II, pp. 91-92).

41. A deputation consisting of ten men came to Medina from Khaulan in the year AH 10. They informed the Prophet

that they were Muslims. The Prophet asked, "What about your idol of 'Amm Anas?." They replied, "That is in a bad shape. We have exchanged him for Allah whom you have brought. When we go back, we shall destroy him." The Prophet ordered some one to instruct them in the Quran and the Traditions. After some days, at the time of their departure, the Prophet ordered that each one of them be given twelve and a half ounces of silver as reward. They went back and destroyed the idol of 'Amm Anas even before they untied their baggage. (Ibid., p. 100).

JIHĀD

1. Fight in the cause of Allah those who fight you ... and slay them wherever you catch them, and turn them out from where they have turned you out; for tumult and oppression are worse than slaughter ... such is the reward of those who suppress faith. But if they cease, Allah is oft-forgiving, most merciful. And fight them on until there is no more tumult or oppression, and there prevails justice and faith in Allah. But if they cease, let there be no hostility except to those who practise oppression. (Quran, 2:190-193).

2. Fighting is prescribed for you, and you dislike it. But it is possible that you dislike a thing which is good for you, and that you love a thing which is bad for you. But Allah knows and you know not... Those who believed and those who suffered exile and fought (and strove and struggled) in the path of Allah — they have the hope of the mercy of Allah. (Quran, 2:216, 218)

3. How many of the Prophets fought (in Allah's way), and with them (fought) large bands of godly men? But they never lost-heart if they met with disaster in Allah's way, nor did they weaken (in will) nor give in. And Allah loves those who are firm and steadfast. All that they said was: "Our Rabb!... establish our feet firmly and help us against those that resist Faith.".... Soon shall we cast terror into the hearts of the

Unbelievers, for that they joined companions with Allah, for which He had sent no authority: their abode will be the Fire: and evil is the home of the wrong-doers! ... And if you are slain, or die, in the way of Allah, forgiveness and mercy from Allah are far better than all they could amass. And if you die, or are slain, Lo! it is unto Allah that you are brought together... Think not of those who are slain in Allah's way as dead. Nay, they live, finding their sustenance in the Presence of their Rabb. (Quran, 3:146-147, 151, 157-158, 169)

4. Let those fight in the cause of Allah who sell the life of this world for the hereafter. To him who fights in the cause of Allah, — whether he is slain or gets victory — soon shall we give him a reward of great (value)... Those who believe fight in the cause of Allah, and those who reject Faith fight in the cause of Tāghūt. So fight you against the Friends of Satan: feeble indeed is the cunning of Satan... Say: "Short is the enjoyment of this world: the Hereafter is the best...! Wherever you are, death will find you out, even if you are in towers built up strong and high!"... He who obeys the Apostle, obeys Allah... Then fight in Allah's cause. You are held responsible only for yourself — and rouse the Believers. It may be that Allah will restrain the fury of the Unbelievers; for Allah is the strongest in might and punishment... They but wish that you should reject Faith, as they do, and thus be on the same footing (as they): but take not friends from their ranks until they flee in the way of Allah (from what is forbidden). But if they turn renegades, seize them and slay them wherever you find them... Never should a Believer kill a Believer... O you who believe! when you go abroad in the cause of Allah... With Allah are profits and spoils abundant. (Quran, 4:74, 76-78, 80, 84, 89, 92-94)

5. O you who believe! Do your duty to Allah, seek the means of approach unto Him, and strive with might and main in His cause that you may prosper... O you who believe! If any from among you turn back from his Faith, soon will Allah produce a people whom He will love as they will love Him, —

lowly with the Believers, mighty against the Rejecters, fighting in the way of Allah, and never afraid of the reproaches. (Quran, 5:38, 57)

6. Those who believe, and adopt exile, and fight for the Faith, in the cause of Allah... for them is the forgiveness of sins and a provision most generous. (Quran, 8:74)

7. Those who believe, and suffer exile and strive with might and main in Allah's cause, with their goods and persons, have the highest rank in the sight of Allah. They are the people who will achieve (salvation). Their Allah does give them glad tidings of a mercy from Himself, of His good pleasure, and of Gardens for them wherein are delights that endure. They will dwell therein for ever. Verily in Allah's presence is a reward, greatest (of all). (Quran, 9:20-22)

8. Go you forth (whether equipped) lightly or heavily, and strive and struggle, with your goods and your persons, in the cause of Allah. That is best for you, if you (but) knew... Those who were left behind (in the Tabūk expedition) rejoiced in their inaction behind the back of the Apostle of Allah: they hated to strive and fight, with their goods and their persons, in the cause of Allah: they said, "Go not forth in the heat." Say, "The fire of Hell is fiercer in heat." If only they could understand! Let them laugh a little: much will they weep: a recompense for the (evil) that they do. (Quran, 9:41, 81-82)

9. Allah has purchased of the Believers their persons and their goods; for theirs (in return) is the Garden (of Paradise): They fight in His cause, and slay and are slain: a promise binding on Him in Truth, through the Taurah, the Injil, and the Quran: And who is more faithful to his covenant than Allah? Then rejoice in the bargain which you have concluded: that is the achievement supreme. (Quran, 9:111)

10. Therefore when you meet the Unbelievers (in fight), smite at their necks; at length, when you have thoroughly subdued them, bind a bond firmly (on them): thereafter (is the time for) either generosity or ransom: until the war lays down its burdens. Thus (are you commanded)... But those who are

slain in the way of Allah — He will never let their deeds be lost. Soon will He guide them and improve their condition, and admit them to the Garden which He has announced for them. O you who believe! If you will aid (the cause of) Allah, He will aid you, and plant your feet firmly. But those who reject (Allah), — for them is destruction... Those who reject Allah and hinder (men) from the path of Allah, then die rejecting Allah, — Allah will not forgive them. (Quran, 47:4-8, 34)

11. Remember your Rabb inspired the angels (with the message): "I am with you: give firmness to the Believers: I will instil terror into the hearts of the Unbelievers: smite you above their necks and smite all their finger-tips off them." This because they contended against Allah and His Apostle: if any contend against Allah and His Apostle, Allah is strict in punishment. Thus (will it be said): "Taste you then of the (punishment): for those who resist Allah, is the penalty of the Fire." (Quran, 8:12-14)

12. Say to the Unbelievers, if (now) they desist (from Unbelief), their past will be forgiven them; but if they persist, the punishment of those before them is already (a matter of warning for them). And fight them on until there is no more tumult and there prevail justice and faith in Allah altogether and everywhere. But if they cease, verily Allah does see all that they do. (Quran, 8:38-39)

13. O Apostle ! rouse the Believers to the fight. If there are twenty among you, patient and persevering, they will vanquish two hundred: if a hundred, they will vanquish a thousand of the Unbelievers: for these are a people without understanding. (Quran, 8:65)

14. Go you [Pagans], then, for four months, backwards and forwards, (as you will), throughout the land. But know you that you cannot frustrate Allah (by your falsehood) but that Allah will cover with shame those who reject Him... But when the forbidden months are past, then fight and slay the Pagans wherever you find them, and seize them, beleaguer them, and

lie in wait for them in every stratagem (of war); but if they repent, and establish regular prayers and practise regular charity, then open the way for them... (Quran, 9:2, 5)

15. Fight those who believe not in Allah nor the Last Day, nor hold that forbidden which has been forbidden by Allah and His Apostle, nor acknowledge the Religion of Truth, (even if they are) of the People of the Book, until they pay the *Jizya* with willing submission and feel themselves subdued... O Prophet ! strive hard against the Unbelievers and Hypocrites, and be firm against them. Their abode is Hell, — an evil refuge indeed... When a Sūra comes down, informing them to believe in Allah and to strive and fight along with His Apostle, those with wealth and influence among them ask you for exemption... But the Apostle, and those who believe with him, strive and fight with their wealth and their persons: for them are (all) good things: and it is they who will prosper. Allah has prepared for them Gardens under which rivers flow, to dwell therein: that is the supreme felicity... O you who believe! Fight the Unbelievers who gird you about, and let them find firmness in you: and know that Allah is with those who fear Him. (Quran, 9:29, 73, 86, 88, 89, 123)

16. Therefore listen not to the Unbelievers, but strive against them with utmost strenuousness, with the (Quran). (Quran, 25:52)

17. And Allah turned back the Unbelievers for (all) their fury: no advantage did they gain; and enough is Allah for the Believers in their fight... And those of the people of the Book who aided them — Allah did take them down from their strongholds and cast terror in their hearts, (so that) some you slew, and some you made prisoners. And He made you heirs of their lands, their houses, and their goods, and of a land which you had not frequented (before). And Allah has power over all things. (Quran, 33:25-27)

18. Against them make ready your strength to the utmost of your power, including steeds of war, to strike terror into (the

hearts of) the enemies of Allah and your enemies... Whatever you shall spend in the cause of Allah, shall be repaid unto you, and you shall not be treated unjustly. (Quran 8:60)

SLAUGHTER

The Bible

1. Moses said to the people, "... May Jehovah, the Elohim of your ancestors, make you increase a thousand times more and make you prosperous, as he promised ... But king Sihon would not let us pass through his country. Jehovah your Elohim had made him stubborn and rebellious, so that we could defeat him and take his territory, which we still occupy. Then Jehovah said to me, 'Look, I have made king Sihon and his land helpless before you; take his land and occupy it.' Sihon came out with all his men to fight us near the town of Jahaz, but Jehovah our Elohim put him in our power, and we killed him, his sons and all his men. At the same time we captured and destroyed every town, and put everyone to death, men women, and children. We left no survivors. We took the livestock and plundered the town. (Deuteronomy, 1:9-11; 2:30-35)

2. "When you go to attack a city, first give its people a chance to surrender. If they open the gates and surrender, they are all to become your slaves and do forced labour for you. But if the people of that city will not surrender, but choose to fight, surround it with your army. Then when Jehovah your Elohim lets you capture the city, kill every man in it. You may, however, take for your slaves the women, the children, the livestock, and every thing else in the city. You may use every thing that belongs to your enemies. Jehovah has given it to you. That is how you are to deal with those cities that are far away from the land you will settle in. (Deuteronomy, 20:10-15)

3. "But when you capture the cities in the land that Jehovah your Elohim is giving you, kill everyone. Completely destroy all the people: the Hittites, the Amorites, the Canaanites, the

Perizzites, the Hivites, and the Jebusites, as Jehovah ordered you to do. Kill them, so that they will not make you sin against Jehovah by teaching you to do all the disgusting things that they do in the worship of their gods. (Deuteronomy, 20:16-18)

The Quran

4. The punishment of those who wage war against Allah and His Apostle, and strive with might and main for mischief through the land is: execution, or crucifixion, or the cutting off of hands and feet from opposite sides, or exile from the land: that is their disgrace in this world, and a heavy punishment is theirs in the Hereafter; except for those who repent before they fall into your power: in that case, know that Allah is oft-forgiving, most merciful. (Quran, 5:36-37)

5. It is not fitting for an Apostle that he should have prisoners of war until he has committed slaughter in the land... O Apostle! say to those who are captives in your hands: If Allah finds any good in your hearts, He will give you something better than what has been taken from you and He will forgive you: for Allah is oft-forgiving, most merciful. But if they have treacherous designs against you, (O Apostle!), they have already been in treason against Allah, and so has He given (you) power over them... (Quran, 8:70-71)

Sunnah of the Prophet of Islam

6. Then the apostle began his return journey to Medina with the unbelieving prisoners, among whom were 'Uqba ... and al-Naḍr. The apostle carried with him the booty that had been taken from the polytheists... Then the apostle went forward until when he came out of the pass of al-Safrā he halted on the sand hill between the pass and al-Nāziya called Sayar at a tree there and divided the booty which Allah had granted to the Muslims equally... When the apostle was in al-Safrā, al-Naḍr was killed by 'Ali, as the learned Meccan told me. When he was in 'Irqu'l-Zebya 'Uqba was killed. He had been captured by 'Abdullah... When the apostle ordered him to be killed

'Uqba said, 'But who will look after my children, Muhammad? 'Hell', he said, and Āsim ... killed him. (Ibn Ishāq, p. 308).

7. When the apostle came to Banū Qurayza he halted by one of their wells near their property called The well of Anā. The men joined him... The apostle besieged them for twenty-five nights until they were sore pressed and Allah cast terror in their hearts... In the morning they submitted to the apostle's judgement... Then they surrendered, and the apostle confined them in Medina. Then the apostle went out to the market of Medina (which is still its market today) and dug trenches in it. Then he sent for them and struck off their heads in those trenches as they were brought out to him in batches. Among them was the enemy of Allah Huyayy and Ka'b b. Asad, their chief. There were 600 or 700 in all, though some put the figure as high as 800 or 900... This went on until the apostle made an end of them... Only one of their women was killed... (Ibn Ishāq, p. 461, 463).

8. A tradition says, " In whatever settlement you do not hear the *azān* or see no mosque, slaughter the people of that place." (*Tabqāt-i-Ibn Sa'd*, Volume I, p. 488.)

ENSLAVEMENT

The Quran:

1. O Prophet! We have made lawful to you your wives to whom you have paid their dowers; and those whom your right hand possesses out of the prisoners of war whom Allah has assigned to you... For the Believers (at large), We know what We have appointed for them as to their wives and the captives whom their right hands possess in order that there should be no difficulty for you... It is not lawful for you (to marry more) women after this, nor to change them for (other) wives, even though their beauty attract you, except any your right hand should possess... (Quran, 33:50, 52)

2. Also (prohibited are) women already married, except those whom your right hands possess: thus has Allah ordained (prohibitions) against you... (Quran, 4:24)

3. If any of you have not the means wherewith to wed free believing women, they may wed believing girls from among those whom your right hands possess: and Allah has full knowledge about your Faith... (Quran, 4:25)

4. The Believers must (eventually) win through, — those who humble themselves in their prayers... who abstain from sex, except with those joined to them in the marriage bond, or (the captives) whom your right hands possess, — for (in their case) they are free from blame. (Quran, 23:1-6)

5. Marry those among you who are single, or the virtuous ones among your slaves, male or female... (Quran, 24:32).

6. And those who guard their chastity, except with their wives and the (captives) whom their right hands possess, — for (then) they are not to be blamed)... (Quran, 70:29-30)

Sunnah of the Prophet of Islam

7. Then the apostle divided the property, wives and children of Banū Qurayza among the Muslims, and he made known on that day the shares of horse and men, and took out the fifth... Then the apostle sent Sa'd... with some of the captive women of Banū Qurayza and he sold them for horses and weapons... Allah sent down concerning the trench and Banū Qurayza the account which is found in the *sūra* of the Confederates. (Ibn Ishāq, 466).

Muhammadan Law

8. Slave Traffic [buying and selling of slaves] is not only allowed but legislated for by Muhammadan law, and is clearly sanctioned by the example of the Prophet as given in the Traditions (see *Sahih Muslim, Kitabu'l-Buyū'*, vol. I, p. 2). In the Law of Sale (see *Raddu'l-Muhtār, Hidayah*, Hamilton's ed., vol. II, p. 458), slaves, male and female, are treated merely as articles of merchandise. In chapters on sale, and option, and wills, the illustrations are generally given as regards slaves, and the same, or very similar, rules apply both to the sale of animals and bondsmen.

The following traditions (*Mishkāt*, book xiii, chapter xx) with reference to the action of the Prophet in this matter are notable:-

"Imrān ibn al-Husain said a man freed six slaves at his death, and he had no other property besides; and the Prophet called them, and divided them into three sections, and then cast lots; he then ordered that two of them should be freed, and he retained four in slavery, and spoke severely of the man who had set them free."

"Jābir said we used to sell the mothers of children in the time of the Prophet, and of Abū Bakr..." (*Dictionary of Islam*, p. 598)

9. The Imam, with respect to captives, has it in his choice to slay them, because the Prophet put captives to death, – and also, because slaying them terminates wickedness: – Or, if he chose, he may make them slaves, because by enslaving them the evil of them is remedied, at the same time that the Mussalmans reap an advantage: – or, if he please, he may release them so as to make them freemen and Zimmees, according to what is recorded of Umar: – but it is not lawful so to release the idolaters of Arabia, or apostates.

It is not lawful for the Imam to return the captives to their own country, as this would be strengthening the infidels against the Mussalmans.

If captives become Mussalmans, let not the Imam put them to death, because the evil of them is here remedied without slaying them, but yet he may lawfully make them slaves, after their conversion, because the reason for making them slaves, (namely, there being secured within the Mussalman territory,) had existence previous to their embracing the faith [of Islam]. It is otherwise where infidels become Mussalmans before their capture, because then the reason for making them slaves did not exist previous to their conversion.

It is not lawful to confer a favour upon captives by releasing them gratuitously, — that is without receiving anything in return, or their becoming Zimmees, or being made slaves.

Shafei says that showing favour to captives, in this way, is lawful, because the Prophet showed favour, in this way, to some of the captives taken at the battle of Biddir. The arguments of our doctors upon this point are two-fold: first, (Allah) says in the Koran: "Slay the idolaters wherever you find them; [Quran, 9:5];" secondly, the right of enslaving them is established by their being conquered and captured, and hence it is not lawful to annul that right without receiving some advantage in return, in the same manner as holds with respect to all plunder; and in respect to what Shafei relates, that "the Prophet showed "favour, in this way, to some of the captives taken at the battle of Biddir," it is abrogated by the text of the Koran already quoted. (*The Hedaya*, pp. 160-161)

10. If a person purchase a female slave (for instance) by an invalid contract, and take possession of her, and the seller take possession of the purchase money, and the purchaser then dispose of her, by sale, to another person at a profit, it is in that case incumbent on him to bestow in charity the profit so acquired: – but if the first seller should have acquired a profit upon, or by means of, the profit money, he is not required to bestow such profit in charity.

The reason for this distinction is that as the female slave (for instance) is a definite article, the second contract of sale relates identically to her, and the profit acquired by the sale of her is accordingly safe. (*The Hedaya*, p. 458)

PLUNDER

The Bible:

1. Jehovah said to Moses, "You and Eleazar, together with the other leaders of the community, are to count everything that has been captured, including the prisoners and the animals. Divide what was taken into two equal parts, one part for the soldiers and the other part for the rest of the community. From the part that belongs to the soldiers, withhold as a tax for Jehovah one out of every five hundred

prisoners and the same proportion of the cattle, donkeys, sheep, and goats. Give them to Eleazar the priest as a special contribution to Jehovah. From the part given to the rest of the people, take one out of every fifty prisoners and the same proportion of the cattle, donkeys, sheep, and goats. Give them to the Levites who are in charge of Jehovah's Tent." Moses and Eleazar did what Jehovah commanded.

The following is the list of what was captured by the soldiers, in addition to what they kept for themselves: 675,000 sheep and goats, 72,000 cattle, 61,000 donkeys, and 32,000 virgins. The half share of the soldiers was 337,500 sheep and goats, of which 675 were the tax for Jehovah; 36,000 cattle for the soldiers, of which 72 were the tax for Jehovah; 30,5000 donkeys for the soldiers, of which 61 were the tax for Jehovah; and 16,000 virgins for the soldiers, of which 32 were the tax for Jehovah. So Moses gave Eleazar the tax as a special contribution to Jehovah, as Jehovah had commanded.

The share of the community was the same as that for the soldiers: 337,500 sheep and goats, 36,000 cattle, 30,500 donkey, and 16,000 virgins. From this share Moses took one out of every fifty prisoners and animals, and as Jehovah had commanded, gave them to the Levites who were in charge of Jehovah's Tent.

Then the officers who had commanded the army went to Moses and reported, "Sir, we have counted the soldiers under our command and not one of them is missing. So we are bringing the gold ornaments, armlets, bracelets, rings, earring, and necklaces that each of us has taken. We offer them to Jehovah as a payment for our lives, so that he will protect us. Moses and Eleazar received the gold, all of which was in the form of ornaments. The total contribution of the officers weighed nearly two hundred kilogrammes. Those who were not officers kept the loot they had taken. So Moses and Eleazar took the gold to the Tent, so that Jehovah would protect the people of Israel. (Numbers, 31:25-54)

The Quran

2. They ask you concerning (thing taken as) spoils of war. Say: "(Such) spoils are at the disposal of Allah and the Apostle: So fear Allah, and keep straight the relations between yourselves: obey Allah and His Apostle, if you do believe." (Quran, 8:1)

3. And know that out of all the booty that you may acquire, (in war) a fifth share is assigned to Allah and to the Apostle, and to near relatives, orphans, the needy, and the wayfarer, — if you do believe in Allah and in the revelation We sent down to Our Servant on the Day of Testing, — the Day of the meeting of the two forces. For Allah has power over all things. (Quran, 8:41)

4. And those of the People of the Book [the Jews] who aided them — Allah did take them down from their strongholds and cast terror into their hearts. (So that) some you slew, and some you made prisoners. And He made you heirs of their lands, their houses, and their goods and of a land which you had not frequented (before). And Allah has power over all things. (Quran, 33:26-27)

ZIMMIS

1. Fight those who believe not in Allah nor the Last Day, nor hold that forbidden which has been forbidden by Allah and His Apostle, nor acknowledge the Religion of Truth, (even if they are) of the People of the Book, until they pay the *Jizya* with willing submission, and feel themselves subdued. (Quran, 9:29)

2. Zimmi is "a member of the Ahlu'z-Zimmah, a non-Muslim subject of a Muslim government, belonging to the Jewish, Christian, or Sabean creed, who for the payment of a poll- or capitation-tax, enjoys security of his person and property in a Muhammadan country". (*Dictionary of Islam*, p. 710)

3. Jizya, or capitation-tax is of two kinds. The first species is that which is established voluntarily, and by composition, — the rate of which is such as may be agreed upon by both parties, — because the Prophet entered into a composition with the tribe of Binney Bifran, for 1200 pieces of cloth, and not more... The second species is that which the Imam himself imposes, when he conquers infidels and then confirms them in their possessions, the common rate of which is fixed by his imposing upon every person in middling circumstances, 24 *dirms* per annum or 2 *dirms* per month; — and upon the labouring poor 12 *dirms* per annum, or 1 *dirm* per month. This is according to our doctors. Shafei maintains that he should exact from each sane and adult person, 1 *deenar*, or something to that amount; — and the poor and wealthy are on an equal footing in this point; because the Prophet said to Maaz, "Take from every male, and female adult 1 *deenar*, or cloth to that value;"... If Mussulman army subdue an infidel territory before any capitation-tax be established, the inhabitants, together with their wives and children, are all plunder, and the property of the State, as it is lawful to reduce to slavery all infidels, whether they be Kitabees, Majoosees or idolaters. (*The Hedaya*, pp. 211, 213)

Disabilities imposed on Zimmis

1. They will not build new idol temples.
2. They will not rebuild any existing temple which may have fallen into disrepair.
3. Muslim travellers will not be prevented from staying in temples.
4. Muslim travellers will be provided hospitality by Zimmis in their own houses for three days.
5. Zimmis will neither act as spies nor give spies shelter in their houses.
6. If any relation of a Zimmi is inclined towards Islam, he should not be prevented from doing so.
7. Zimmis will respect Muslims.

8.   Zimmis will courteously receive a Muslim wishing to attend their meetings.

9.   Zimmis will not dress like Muslims.

10.   They will not take Muslim names.

11.   They will not ride horses with saddle and bridle.

12.   They will not possess swords, bows or arrows.

13.   They will not wear signet rings

14.   They will not openly sell or drink intoxicating liquor.

15.   They will not abandon their traditional dress, which is a sign of their ignorance, in order that they may be distinguished from Muslims.

16.   They will not openly practise their traditional customs amongst Muslims.

17.   They will not build their houses in the neighbourhood of Muslims.

18.   They will not carry or bury their dead near Muslim graveyards.

19.   They will not mourn their dead loudly.

20.   They will not buy Muslim slaves.

(*Zakhiratu'l-Muluk,* pp. 117-18 quoted in *A History of Sufisim in India*, pp. 295-96).